631.5 ROB
Roberts, Jack L.
Organic agriculture

NORFOLK PUBLIC L
NORFOLK, NEBR/

D0860109

USA TODAY'S DEBATE: VOICES AND PERSPECTIVES

ORGANIC AGRICULTURE

Protecting Our Food Supply or Chasing Imaginary Risks?

Jack L. Roberts

Twenty-First Century Books · Minneapolis

USA TODAY®, its logo, and associated graphics are federally registered trademarks. All rights are reserved. All USA TODAY text, graphic, and photographs are used pursuant to a license and may not be reproduced, distributed, or otherwise used without the express written consent of Gannett Co., Inc.

USA TODAY Snapshots®, graphics, and excerpts from USA TODAY articles quoted on back cover and on pages 11, 20–21, 28, 32–33, 42–43, 44, 54–55, 58, 72–73, 74, 76, 88–89, 92, 95, 98–99 © copyright 2012 by USA TODAY.

Copyright © 2012 by Lerner Publishing Group, Inc.

All rights reserved. International copyright secured. No part of this book may be reproduced, stored in a retrieval system, or transmitted in any form or by any means—electronic, mechanical, photocopying, recording, or otherwise—without the prior written permission of Lerner Publishing Group, Inc., except for the inclusion of brief quotations in an acknowledged review.

Twenty-First Century Books
A division of Lerner Publishing Group, Inc.
241 First Avenue North
Minneapolis, MN 55401 U.S.A.

Website address: www.lernerbooks.com

Library of Congress Cataloging-in-Publication Data

Roberts, Jack L.
    Organic agriculture : protecting our food supply or chasing imaginary risks? / by Jack L. Roberts.
        p.   cm.—(USA today's debate: voices and perspectives)
    Includes bibliographical references and index.
    ISBN 978–0–7613–6434–4 (lib. bdg. : alk. paper)
    1. Organic farming. 2. Natural foods. I. Title. II. Series: USA today's debate.
   S605.5.R59 2012
   631.5'84—dc22   2011000188

Manufactured in the United States of America
1 – MG – 7/15/11

CONTENTS

INTRODUCTION

The Organic Agriculture Debate

O N THE FIRST DAY OF SPRING IN 2009, THE FIRST LADY of the United States, Michelle Obama, planted a 1,100-square-foot (102-square-meter) organic vegetable garden on the White House lawn. The goal was simple. She wanted to grow a variety of vegetables, berries, and herbs. Her plan was to use only natural fertilizers and pest control methods. All the crops would be used by the White House chefs in preparing meals for both family dinners and formal White House events.

This wasn't the first time a first lady had planted a garden on the White House lawn. Eleanor Roosevelt was the wife of the thirty-second president of the United States, Franklin Delano Roosevelt. She planted a vegetable and herb garden on the White House lawn during World War II (1939–1945). She called it a Victory Garden. The First Lady encouraged all Americans to plant their own Victory Gardens to support the war effort. In the 1990s, Hillary Clinton, wife

Left: Students garden with First Lady Michelle Obama, planting herbs in the organic White House garden in 2009.

of the forty-second president, Bill Clinton, planted a vegetable garden on the roof of the White House.

Most people found Michelle Obama's organic vegetable garden a good idea. Some, however, found it troubling. They wondered why she chose to plant and promote an *organic* garden.

One of these is Bonnie McCarvel, executive director of the Mid America CropLife Association. The mission of her organization is to provide information about the safety and value of American agricultural food production—*conventional* agriculture.

McCarvel wrote to First Lady Obama to remind her of the importance of conventional farming. "As you go about planning and planting the White House garden," McCarvel wrote, "we respectfully encourage you to recognize the role conventional agriculture plays in the U.S." She went on to point out that conventional agriculture feeds an ever-increasing world population. It also contributes to the U.S. economy. Finally, it provides a safe and economical food supply.

FACT OR FICTION?

The controversy created by the simple act of planting a White House garden illustrates an important issue. In the twenty-first century, people around the world are engaged in a heated debate over organic versus conventional agriculture. The two sides are sharply divided.

On one hand, many believe organic food is safer and more nutritious than conventionally grown food. They also believe that organic agriculture is better for the environment and for the health and well-being of livestock and crops. They argue that conventional farmers have too little regard for the environment. They also say that conventional farmers are interested only in producing the largest crops (or the fattest cattle) for the biggest profits.

Conventional farmers and industry leaders disagree with those claims. They say scientific evidence does not support the idea that organic farming is superior in any way to conventional farming. They also believe organic-farming advocates unfairly question the safety of conventionally grown products. Proponents of conventional farming say, for example, that the United Kingdom's Soil Association makes unfair statements. The Soil Association says conventional agriculture's use of pesticides and insecticides

Above: This coffee has been certified organic by the nonprofit Soil Association. The charity is the largest organic organization in the United Kingdom.

is dangerous. These chemicals "are the only substances that are deliberately released into the environment designed to kill living things," the association states. "They pose unique hazards to human health and the environment."

But Nina Fedoroff, science and technology adviser to the U.S. secretary of state, disagrees. Fedoroff believes organic agriculture is a marketing tool, not a safety measure. She says that the marketing of organic food products is designed simply to allow farmers to charge more for those products. In a 2009 article for *Seed* magazine, she wrote about what she calls agri-myths. One of those myths, she says, is that organic food is better for you and the land because it is grown with manure instead of chemicals. This, Fedoroff says, is not true. "Nitrogen [an element important to plant life] is nitrogen—but it's pretty good marketing if you're selling poor produce at exorbitant prices."

Above: **A crop duster, or agricultural plane used to spray crops, lays down a cloud of synthetic pesticides.**

Who is right? Is organic agriculture safer than conventional agriculture? To answer that question, we need to have a better understanding of what organic agriculture is. How does it differ from conventional agriculture? In a nutshell, organic agriculture is farming without the use of conventional fertilizers and synthetic pesticides. Organic agriculture does not use growth hormones or antibiotics in raising livestock. But that's really only part of the definition.

The Organic Trade Association is a nonprofit organization whose mission is to promote and protect organic trade to benefit the environment, farmers, the public, and the economy. The association says organic agriculture involves an integrated system. It includes production, processing, and distribution of food. This system is regulated by strict national guidelines. These guidelines were established by the U.S. Department of Agriculture (USDA). They are designed to assure consumers that food products labeled *organic* are grown and processed under these guidelines.

In other words, organic farming does not simply avoid the use of insecticides, pesticides, and synthetic hormones for livestock. As the USDA's National Institute of Food and Agriculture explains, it also involves putting into practice a wide range of strategies. As well as producing healthy food, these strategies help develop and maintain biological diversity and renew soil fertility.

According to some organic food supporters, these strategies are critical to the well-being of the United States and the world. Maria Rodale is one of those organic food advocates. Rodale is chief executive officer and chairman of Rodale Inc., a multimedia company that declares its focus to be on "health, wellness, and the environment." She is also the granddaughter of the founder of the organic movement in the United States, J. I. Rodale.

Recently, Maria Rodale wrote a book titled *Organic Manifesto: How Organic Farming Can Heal Our Planet, Feed the World, and Keep Us Safe.* In it, she says organic agriculture is the only way the human race

> **We are all being poisoned, contaminated, sterilized, and eventually exterminated by the synthetic chemicals we have used for the last 100 years to grow our food and maintain our lawns, to make our lives easier and 'cleaner' and our food 'cheaper.'**

–**MARIA RODALE,** CEO AND CHAIRMAN, RODALE INC., 2010

will survive on this planet. "We are all being poisoned, contaminated, sterilized, and eventually exterminated by the synthetic chemicals we have used for the last 100 years to grow our food and maintain our lawns, to make our lives easier and 'cleaner' and our food 'cheaper.'"

To many on the opposite side of the debate, the idea that conventional farming will exterminate the human race is laughable. Instead, conventional agriculturists argue that modern agricultural technology is the only way to save the planet. The world's population is almost seven billion people. By the year 2050, it is expected to grow to nine billion. Conventional agriculturists believe it would be impossible to feed the world without using conventional farming practices. "If everybody switched to organic farming," Fedoroff says flatly, "we couldn't support the earth's current population—maybe half."

THE LARGER DEBATE

The debate over organic farming versus conventional farming is complicated, with many questions to examine. For example, is organic farming really safer for the environment than conventional farming? Is organic food more nutritious and better for your health than conventional food?

What about the economic issues? Is organic food, which is usually more expensive, really worth the additional cost?

Social issues are part of the debate too. Do organic farmers treat livestock better and more humanely than conventional farmers? And is organic

> ❝ **If everybody switched to organic farming, we couldn't support the earth's current population—maybe half.** ❞

–**NINA FEDOROFF,** SCIENCE AND TECHNOLOGY ADVISER TO THE U.S. SECRETARY OF STATE, 2008

Conventional vs. Organic Farming: At-a-Glance

	Conventional farming	Organic farming
Pest control	Sprays pesticides to reduce pests and disease	Introduces beneficial insects; uses traps to catch pests
Weed control	Uses chemical herbicides to kill weeds	Rotates crops; tills; hand weeds
Livestock management/ growth	Gives animals antibiotics, growth hormones, medications; often confines animals	Feeds animals organic feed; allows animals to roam and graze free; provides clean housing to minimize disease
Plant growth	Uses chemical fertilizers to promote growth	Employs natural fertilizers, such as manure and compost to fertilize the soil

food a real alternative for the entire world, not just for wealthy developed nations?

So who is right? Are we protecting our food supply or trying to avoid imaginary risks? Can organic and conventional farming ever live peacefully and productively side by side? To find out, we must carefully evaluate the facts.

USA TODAY Snapshots®

Shoppers who said at least 25% of their food purchases are natural and/or organic

2010
27%

2009
20%

Source: Harris Interactive survey of 3,484 adults for Whole Foods Market conducted online June 24–29

By Michelle Healy and Karl Gelles, USA TODAY, 2010

CHAPTER ONE

The Roots of Organic Agriculture

THE HISTORY OF ORGANIC AGRICULTURE BEGINS more than a century ago. It focuses on a few activists in Great Britain and the United States who believed human health was dependent upon healthy soil. Throughout much of the twentieth century, their philosophies met strong opposition, even ridicule. But in the United States, their work resulted in the development of strict guidelines for the production and processing of food labeled *organic*. The USDA adopted these standards in 2002. The U.S. government's National Organic Program (NOP) enforces them.

The road that led to the establishment of these standards was long and often difficult. The story still stirs up debate among scientists, food producers, and consumers. It had several significant milestones.

Left: A horticulturist at work in the fields of Pennsylvania's Rodale Institute in 2009. Founded in 1947 by J. I. Rodale, the nonprofit Rodale Institute is among the world's leading organic organizations.

THE 1800S

Most historians say the history of the organic food movement began more than 150 years ago. That's when German chemist Justus von Liebig (1803–1873) identified three major chemicals that plants need to grow: nitrogen (N), phosphorus (P), and potassium (K). Before this discovery, the major source of these important nutrients was humus.

Above: German chemist Justus von Liebig invented the first synthetic fertilizer. Liebig is known as the father of the fertilizer industry.

Humus is the decayed remains of once-living plants and animals. Since the beginning of agriculture, humus has been a natural, or organic, fertilizer for soil.

Fertilization is critical to healthy crops. It improves soil quality which, in turn, improves soil fertility. Ultimately, it improves the growth and yield of crops.

Liebig realized that natural fertilizers could be replaced or improved by chemical (inorganic) fertilizers. He created a nitrogen-based synthetic fertilizer, a major development for agriculture. This eventually led to widespread use throughout the world of inorganic fertilizers. For his discovery, Liebig is recognized as the father of the fertilizer industry.

THE DEBATE BEGINS

By 1918, at the end of World War I (1914–1918), many farmers had begun to use chemical fertilizers to improve the fertility of the soil. At the same time, a few organic agriculture pioneers were becoming concerned. They believed chemical fertilizers damaged the soil. They considered chemical fertilizers to be harmful to the production of food.

One of the most outspoken advocates for healthier soil was a botanist from Great Britain. His name was Sir Albert Howard (1873–1947). Between 1924 and 1931, Howard developed a sophisticated process for converting plant and animal waste into humus. His method increased the soil's organic matter. That, in turn, increased the release of nutrients into the soil.

Howard believed it was essential to keep soil healthy and fertile. To do so, he felt it necessary to recycle all organic waste materials. That included sewage sludge. In 1943 Howard published the book *An Agricultural Testament*. It was about the interrelationship of the health of the soil with the health of plants, animals, and humans. Howard wrote that all living things are dependent upon the health of the soil.

Howard called the use of chemical fertilizers "fundamentally unsound." He believed the only way to maintain healthy soil was through organic agricultural practices. Humus, not chemistry, was the foundation of healthy soil. Howard wrote: "Artificial manures lead inevitably to artificial nutrition, artificial food, artificial animals, and finally to artificial men and women."

Howard's ideas, however, were not widely accepted. Most farmers and agriculturalists saw chemical fertilizers as a way to increase crop yield. That meant more food at a lower cost. Howard, however, stood firm. He argued that too many farmers were abusing the land, which would ultimately have dire consequences: "The soils of the world are either being worn out and left in ruins, or are being slowly poisoned.... Mother earth has recorded her disapproval by the steady growth of disease in crops, animals, and mankind."

Howard also believed the health of people everywhere could be improved and that a vast number of illnesses could be eliminated by providing food

> " **The soils of the world are either being worn out and left in ruins, or are being slowly poisoned. . . . Mother earth has recorded her disapproval by the steady growth of disease in crops, animals, and mankind.** "
>
> **–SIR ALBERT HOWARD,** *AN AGRICULTURAL TESTAMENT,* 1940

grown from healthy soil. He made a bold forecast. "At least half of the illnesses of mankind will disappear once our food supplies are raised from fertile soil and consumed in a fresh condition." Howard was a pioneer in the development of organic concepts and methods. He is recognized by most agricultural historians as the founder of the organic movement.

CHEMICAL FERTILIZERS AND PESTICIDES

World War II ended in 1945. Suddenly, U.S. factories that had been producing tanks, weapons, and ammunition for the war sat idle. Owners of these plants looked for a new source of income. Many saw potentially big business in the production of chemical fertilizers and pesticides. For example, instead of producing ammonium nitrate for weapons and ammunition, factories could produce ammonium nitrate fertilizer. Military technologies developed for chemical warfare could be redirected for agricultural pesticides.

One class of pesticides that became popular at this time was organophosphates. Still used in the twenty-first century, organophosphates kill insects by attacking their nervous systems. The problem, according to many critics, is that organophosphates can also harm the nervous systems of animals and humans.

Organic or Conventional Farming—a Pioneer's <u>Viewpoint</u>

British farmer and educator Lady Evelyn (Eve) Balfour was a pioneer in the organic agriculture movement. Her work has influenced organic farming throughout the world. In 1939 Lady Eve Balfour launched the Haughley Experiment. This was a thirty-year comparison of organic and conventional farming. In 1946 she founded the Soil Association, the United Kingdom's first organic farming organization.

In 1977 Lady Eve Balfour gave an address at the International Federation of Organic Agriculture Movements (IFOAM) conference in Switzerland. It was titled "Towards a Sustainable Agriculture—The Living Soil." Balfour presented a view of the differences between organic and conventional farming.

She said that the modern farmer sees pests and weeds as an enemy to be exterminated. The modern farmer attacks these pests with chemicals. How these chemicals might affect the food supply is not considered. Neither is the effect the chemicals might have on wildlife. The attitude of the organic farmer, said Balfour, was different. "He tries to see the living world as a whole. He studies what appear to be nature's rules. He attempts to adapt [those rules] to his own farm needs."

Above: Lady Evelyn (Eve) Balfour founded the Soil Association in 1946.

Above: A woman works at a Detroit, Michigan, ammunition factory during World War II. When the war ended, many factories like this began instead to produce pesticides or synthetic fertilizers.

Another chemical marketed for pest control was DDT (dichlorodiphenyltrichloroethane). This chemical had been used effectively during the war to help protect troops from mosquitoes. Mosquito bites could lead to malaria or typhus, potentially deadly diseases.

Soon farmers around the world were using chemical-based insecticides and pesticides. For manufacturers, they were easy to produce. For farmers, they were cost-effective and highly efficient. The new pesticides made it possible for farmers to produce more food on less land. They also needed less human labor. All this meant prices for food could go down. Yet, a small group of activists were increasingly concerned about the potential harmful effects of these chemicals on the environment and on human health.

ORGANIC PIONEER

One of those activists was an American named J. I. Rodale. Rodale was concerned about the growing and processing of food in the United States. In the late 1930s, he had discovered the writings of Albert Howard. Howard's books strongly influenced Rodale's thinking.

In 1940 Rodale purchased a 63-acre (26 hectares) farm in Emmaus, Pennsylvania. He wanted to practice the organic agricultural principles Howard recommended. Two years later, Rodale started a magazine called *Organic Farming and Gardening*. In 1947 he opened the Rodale Institute to study the relationship between healthy soil and healthy food. And in 1950, he began *Prevention* magazine. The magazine is still held in high regard.

Critics dismissed both Rodale and Howard as nothing more than "gloomy prophets." In 1971, for example, the *New York Times* published an article about Rodale. It was titled "Guru of the Organic Food Cult." The author described Rodale as "superstitious, faddish, and unscientific." He said Rodale was obsessed with "an idea whose time had passed, long ago, like the horse drawn plow."

Above: Entrepreneur, publisher, and organic-farming activist J. I. Rodale tastes sunflower seeds in 1970.

With new organic labels, each purchase equals a vote

From the Pages of USA TODAY

I can't do it all. I compost, I recycle and, above all, I buy the food my grocer calls organic. But I admit that I slip my 5-year-old (and myself) a pacifying pizza slice now and again. And no matter what I do for the environment, the carbon dioxide still spews from my tailpipe, and Freon leaks from my air-conditioner, even on treks to the local farmers market.

The government can't do it all, either. It has to regulate all of the chemicals in every breath you take and every gulp you swallow—a lot like a mom's job on a national scale. But it has finally come up with a way to let you know whether what you feed your child is definitely, certifiably good for you.

Notice I didn't say "absolutely" or "irrefutably." After all, the government won't even say "organic" equals "good," but at least purity is no longer in the eye of the beholder. What the Agriculture Department has handed down, effective today, are the first rules for what deserves its "USDA certified organic" label. Any produce provider—from chain store to green-market stall—has to submit to these rules. So must processed-food producers that use organic-only ingredients in their cookies, taco shells or pudding cups.

USDA's requirements

What the government's labs and laws and threats of major punishment will guarantee for American consumers is peace of mind. If you buy anything with the new organic label, you are promised:

- No grower messed with the food's DNA, zapped it with radiation or grew it in sewage sludge.
- The label will be only on produce that wasn't directly sprayed with pesticides and has no more than 5% of the pesticide dosage the Environmental Protection Agency already declares safe (0% isn't possible, because bug killers sprayed elsewhere land on other crops).
- If "organic materials" are in the mix of some prefab goodie, no less than 70% of the ingredients will have been organically grown.

• No labeled livestock or fowl will have been cloned or pumped up with hormones or jolted with preventive antibiotics.

There are other arcane rules that regulators, growers and consumer groups hashed out endlessly. Despite the eye-crossing drudgery, I took some delight in every laborious minute; after all, my family had waited 60 years for organic foods to be thoroughly recognized here.

My grandfather, J. I. Rodale, nurtured a publishing company that was devoted to the "organic" way of life. Led by his vision, many of us planted organic Victory gardens, championed local growers and paid a few extra pennies for purity. We knew this was too important to be just a fad. During the past 10 years, the market for organic food has grown more than 500%, with no signs of slowing.

Grumbles, bumbles likely

I'm delighted by all of the delicious options the organic movement has invented and proud that the government is pointing them out on the shelves. Sure, the growers might grumble and the grocers might bumble and the food processors might have to find new processes. Conventional growers still complain that organic won't work, that it's too labor intensive, not as productive and not practical on a large global scale. But thousands of organic farmers are proving them false, raising reliable crops in huge quantities over massive acreage. Because of them, we have a new chance to treat each purchase as a civic message sent to manufacturers, like casting a vote for a little organic candidate.

That's why I like the whole cause: You can think of yourself as powerless, but when you go into the supermarket, you control the world. Your purchases can literally change the economy, farmers' lives, the environment. With these new federal rules, you can judge companies' products more clearly and know just whom to reward.

Organic-minded consumers hungrily await healthy new bounties—foods that are not just clean and pure, but also quick and easy. Companies will find ready mouths awaiting their organic innovations. Personally, I want to thank the movement for organic, individually wrapped American cheese, which often keeps my child sated (and makes a great grilled cheese). But where's the organic Miracle Whip—light version, please.

We still have a long way to go. Today, I'm just happy we're this far.

—Maria Rodale

Despite the harsh criticism, Rodale was developing a small but loyal group of followers. He changed the name of his organic agriculture magazine to *Organic Gardening.* (More than seventy years later, it is still published.) He began to generate interest in organic farming and organic food. Rodale is said to have popularized the term *organic* to mean "grown without pesticides."

During this time, Rodale declared that eating large quantities of red meat and dairy products dramatically increased the risk of heart disease. Though he was ridiculed for this theory, most twenty-first-century doctors agree. J. I. Rodale died in 1971. Many consider him to be the father of the organic food movement in the United States. As one historian wrote, "Both Howard and Rodale saw the conflict of organic versus non-organic agriculture as a struggle between two different visions of what agriculture should become as they engaged in a war of words with the agricultural establishment."

THE U.S. ENVIRONMENTAL MOVEMENT

In 1962 American biologist Rachel Carson published a book titled *Silent Spring.* The book focused attention on the widespread use (or misuse) of the pesticide DDT. Carson said DDT was being applied without consideration for its harmful effects on humans and wildlife.

Some believe that *Silent Spring,* which was widely read, launched the modern environmental movement. The organic industry began to grow as consumers expressed concerns about the harmful effects of chemical pesticides. The majority of the population, however, considered organic food to be an eccentric fad.

While Rodale was gathering followers (often referred to as "health nuts"), the USDA was generally ignoring organic farming. Even universities that focused on the teaching of agriculture failed to offer classes about organic farming.

One particularly vocal opponent of organic farming at this

> **Before we go back to an organic agriculture in this country, somebody must decide which fifty million Americans we are going to let starve or go hungry.**
>
> **—EARL L. BUTZ,** U.S. SECRETARY OF AGRICULTURE, 1971

Above: Earl L. Butz, secretary of agriculture in the 1970s, was an outspoken advocate of conventional agriculture. Butz was vocal in his opposition to the organic agriculture movement.

time was Earl L. Butz. He was secretary of agriculture from 1971 to 1976 under presidents Richard Nixon and Gerald Ford. Butz declared that organic farming could not produce enough food to feed the nation. In one famous 1971 remark, he said, "Before we go back to an organic agriculture in this country, somebody must decide which fifty million Americans we are going to let starve or go hungry."

REPORT ON ORGANIC FARMING

By the late 1970s, interest in organic farming began to grow, largely because of Robert S. Bergland's support. Bergland was secretary of agriculture during President Jimmy Carter's administration. Having been a farmer in Minnesota, Bergland understood the business. And he believed in the benefits of organic farming.

By this time, many Americans had begun to talk about the need for nationwide standards for the production of food that was to be labeled "organic." In 1979 California passed the first law establishing a legal standard for organic production.

In 1980, under Bergland's direction, the USDA published the *Report and Recommendations on Organic Farming*. This report was based on a study that looked at the potential of organic farming and food production. It called for research and educational support for organic farming. Further, it recommended a comprehensive study be conducted of the economic, social, and environmental results of organic farming versus conventional agriculture. Finally, it suggested the USDA appoint an organic farming coordinator. The report recommended the appointment of a go-between for the USDA and organic farmers and producers. Bergland immediately appointed Garth Youngberg to be the USDA's first organic farming coordinator.

A RETURN TO THE PAST

By 1981, the beginning of President Ronald Reagan's administration, the tide had once again turned away from organic farming in the United States. The new secretary of agriculture was John R. Block. Block flatly dismissed the 1980 report on organic farming and many of its recommendations. He eliminated the position of farming coordinator.

Still, by this time, the United States had more supporters of organic agriculture. They felt consistent standards for food that was labeled organic should be put in place. In the late 1980s, the organic agriculture industry petitioned Congress to establish national guidelines. The industry believed such standards were important in helping consumers understand and have greater confidence in organic foods.

After years of debate, Congress passed the Organic Foods Production Act (OFPA) as part of the 1990 Farm Bill. The act authorized the USDA to establish a National Organic Program (NOP). The program was to regulate national standards for the production, processing, and marketing of organic products. This new policy was considered by many to be an endorsement of organic agriculture.

THE TWENTY-FIRST CENTURY

Between 1997 and 2007, the number of organic farmers increased by 20 percent a year. Some conventional farmers saw the profits in organic farming and switched to organic for financial reasons. Many other conventional farmers switched because they wished to follow the principles of organic farming. They believed that organic farming was better for the land and for livestock. They also believed the quality of organic food was better than food raised through conventional methods. Still, at the end of 2007, organic farmland accounted for less than 2 percent of all farmland in America.

Despite the progress, organic agriculture issues continue to cause political controversy. President Barack Obama's 2009 appointment of Tom Vilsack as thirtieth secretary of the U.S. Department of Agriculture was severely criticized. Many organic proponents felt that Vilsack favored conventional farming, including agribusiness biotech giants such as Monsanto. Yet, according to the website Whorunsgov.com, published by the Washington Post Company, Vilsack "increased funding to support organic farming and family farms" and "teamed up with other agencies to fight childhood obesity and increase food safety."

THE FUTURE

The future of organic agriculture is still unclear. Will agriculturalists change the way they manage the soil and produce food crops? Some observers believe that a compromise between organic and conventional farming proponents could have a positive effect on the future of agriculture.

CHAPTER TWO

Organic Agriculture and the Law

AURORA ORGANIC DAIRY SAYS IT'S A COMPANY WITH priorities. Those priorities are clearly stated in the company's slogan. "From Cow to Carton," the slogan reads, "we produce the highest quality organic milk with affordable pricing." The slogan is featured on the company's website. Next to it is a picture of contented-looking cows grazing in an open pasture. As the company sees it, "healthy, organic cows produce high-quality, delicious organic milk."

Yet, not everyone believes that Aurora is living up to its slogan. Since its founding in 2003, Aurora Organic Dairy often has been involved in controversy and lawsuits. The lawsuits question just how *organic* the company's organic milk and milk products really are. Challengers ask how contented the cows can be when they are allegedly confined to feedlots for much of their lives.

Left: Aurora Organic Dairy cattle graze in open pasture. Lawsuits filed by consumer groups in the early 2000s accused Aurora of confining their cows to feedlots for much of the year.

USA TODAY Snapshots®

Got organic milk?

Organic milk accounts for only 1.2% of the market, but consumption is increasing. Gallons of organic milk purchased in:

In millions　　　　**40.7**

35.1

29.2

2002　　　2003　　　2004[1]

1 – 2004 estimated
Sources: National Dairy Council, Dairy Management Inc.

By Rebecca F. Johnson and Web Bryant, USA TODAY, 2004

One challenger is the Cornucopia Institute. Cornucopia is a Wisconsin-based farm policy research group. In 2005 and 2006, the institute filed formal complaints with the USDA. Cornucopia asked the USDA to investigate alleged violations by Aurora of the law governing food products labeled organic. This is a law that Aurora Dairy cofounder Mark Retzloff helped write.

The complaints focused on one particular part of the federal code. Cornucopia alleged that Aurora's cows were not allowed to graze on open pasture, as required by the law. Instead, they were kept in feedlots. A feedlot is a confined plot of land or pen where livestock are fattened for market.

Aurora denied the allegations. Company officials pointed out that Aurora had been certified organic by the USDA. Retzloff, in particular, was disturbed by the complaints. "When activists challenge the 'organicness' of a certified organic product," he said, "and claim that the USDA National Organic Program or certifiers aren't doing their jobs to ensure the integrity of organic products, the end result is consumer trust will erode and demand will decline." Still, Aurora agreed to make changes to their feedlot operation, as required by the USDA regulations.

This legal action is a good example of the existing tensions between some organic producers and consumer watchdog

> ❝ **When activists challenge the 'organicness' of a certified organic product, and claim that the USDA National Organic Program or certifiers aren't doing their jobs to ensure the integrity of organic products, the end result is consumer trust will erode and demand will decline.** ❞
>
> **–MARK RETZLOFF,** PRESIDENT AND CHIEF "ORGANIC" OFFICER, AURORA ORGANIC DAIRY, 2008

groups. These tensions have existed since the 2002 rules governing organic agriculture were first established.

THE LEGISLATION

The purpose of the 1990 Organic Foods Production Act (OFPA) was to reassure consumers that products marketed as organic met certain standards. When OFPA was passed, Maria Rodale explained, "Until now, it's been up to states and individual companies to monitor the integrity of their organic products. So there was no guarantee that something that was organic in California was as organic as something in Pennsylvania."

The National Organic Program (NOP) created by the OFPA took ten years to create the national organic standards that were finally adopted by the USDA in 2000. These regulations came into full effect in 2002. The regulations explain exactly what farmers must do to have their crops or livestock certified organic. They also require yearly inspections by state-run or private agencies approved by NOP. Among other issues, NOP standards address crop production, livestock management, and packaging and

Above: Businesswoman and environmentalist Maria Rodale is a strong supporter of federal standards for organically produced agricultural products.

handling. Some of the key regulations include these:

Crop production: Organic food crops can only be grown on certain land. That land must be free of any synthetic chemicals for three years prior to growing. These include fertilizers, herbicides, insecticides, or fungicides. Organic producers cannot use any synthetic pesticides or fertilizers in growing the crops. Also, at least 30 feet (9 m) must separate organic land and any conventionally farmed fields. This is to prevent unapproved pesticides from seeping into the organic soil from nearby nonorganic farmland. Finally, no genetically modified (GM) crops are allowed in organic production.

Organic livestock management: Organic farmers cannot give their livestock growth hormones or antibiotics. They cannot give the animals medications, other than vaccinations, unless they are sick. If it is necessary to give an animal an antibiotic, the animal must be removed from the organic herd. That animal can no longer be used for organic production. Nor can it be sold, labeled, or represented as organic.

To be certified organic, animals must eat feed that is 100 percent organic. They must have "access to pasture." This means the animals must have access to fresh air and direct sunlight. Grazing animals must also be able to graze in certified organic pastures.

Poultry farmers must feed their birds organic food and cannot give them antibiotics or other prohibited substances. Finally, an organic livestock farm must keep accurate records of all its animals. The farm must provide the USDA with detailed information about each animal (or, in the case of poultry, each flock). This is to show the same farms are meeting USDA's National Organic Program standards.

Processing and handling: The law also specifies how organic foods are to be processed and packaged. For example, organic products cannot be packaged in anything that contains or has been in contact with synthetic fungicides or preservatives. Certain specific additives are not allowed in organic products.

Below: Dairy cattle roam freely on an organic farm in Maine. To receive organic certification, farmers must allow their cattle access to pasture rather than confining them to feedlots.

Farming on a human scale

From the Pages of
USA TODAY

The white metal sign over the desk at Polyface Farm reads, "Joel Salatin: Lunatic Farmer."

Salatin is proud of that label. "I'm a third-generation lunatic," he boasts while standing in his lush, green central Virginia fields. Brown chickens strut and peck around his feet. "I don't do anything like average farmers do," he says.

What the 52-year-old farmer does is let his cows feed on grass instead of corn or grain. He moves his cows to new fields daily. Flocks of chickens scratch around open fields, spreading cow droppings, eating flies and larvae, and laying eggs in the Salatin-built eggmobile. Hogs forage in the woods or in a pasture house, where they root through cow manure, wood chips and corn. The resulting compost gets spread back over the fields, fertilizing the grass for the cattle. That completes the cycle.

"It's completely counter to current agricultural wisdom," he says. Current agricultural practices often encourage using technology—petroleum-based fertilizers, hormones and antibiotics—to spur growth and reduce costs as much as possible.

Salatin has become known for his unconventional ways. [He] spurns pesticides, antibiotics and fertilizers. "I'm honoring the traditional natural patterns. It's about enhancing the cowness of the cow."

Polyface Farm began in 1961 when Salatin's parents, William and Lucille, bought the 550-acre [223 hectares] property. Salatin took over Polyface in 1982 [and t]he farm remains a family operation. Salatin's wife, Teresa, handles bookkeeping; their son, Daniel, runs the day-to-day operations; Daniel's wife, Sheri, handles marketing.

[Salatin's method of] agriculture remains a tiny fraction of the [American] food supply. "It's a small part, maybe 5 percent," estimates Jean Halloran, director of Food Policy Initiatives at Consumers Union, publisher of the magazine *Consumer Reports.* "But it's rapidly growing."

Critics of this kind of local, all-natural farming have said the food is too expensive and wouldn't work on a large enough scale to feed a hungry nation.

James McWilliams, a professor of agricultural history at the University of Texas–Austin, isn't convinced that local food is the only way to go. Economies of scale [as the amount produced increases, the production cost decreases], when it comes to farming and to transportation, are real, he says. Trains and boats, for example, are efficient ways to move food.

Above: Joel Salatin *(left)* and his son, Daniel, tend to a herd of pigs at Polyface Farm. Salatin practices local, all-natural farming.

Trucks, especially over short distances, are not.

Halloran disagrees with the critics. For one thing, she says, large-scale industrial agriculture has many costs associated with it that aren't reflected in the price of food.

"There are other things that have made industrial food production cheap that are of questionable sustainability," she says. For example, antibiotics are in widespread use at large feedlots, and that contributes to antibiotic-resistant bacteria. "We pay a price for that."

As to the argument that Salatin's methods aren't scalable [could not be applied on much larger farms] and not every farm could operate like Polyface, Halloran says small-scale production can work because cutting the distance between the farm and the consumer will reduce transportation costs, favoring the local farmer. Meanwhile, consumers are starting to place a greater value on the variety and freshness that local farms offer, she says.

Salatin says his farm feeds more people per acre than other farms, though he concedes it requires more labor than most.

To Salatin, his environmental and sustainable approach isn't just the future, it's the moral way to farm.

He puts down a warm, freshly laid egg and strolls through his herd of cattle.

"Hello, people!" he calls out, stopping to stroke the nose of one of his grass-fed cows. "The greatest tragedy," he says, "is that we're abnormal."

–Joshua Hatch

CERTIFIED ORGANIC
LABEL GUIDE

Producers who meet the strict standards set by the NOP may label their products as USDA certified organic. They also may display the official USDA organic seal on their packaging. Products can be labeled organic in one of three ways:

100 percent organic: Foods that have this label are made with 100 percent organic ingredients. They may display the official USDA organic seal.

Organic: Foods labeled as organic must contain at least 95 to 99 percent organic ingredients. The other 5 percent of the ingredients must come from a very specific list of nonorganically produced agricultural products. These are products, such as fish oils and gelatin, that are not available in organic form. Foods labeled organic may also display the official organic seal.

Made with organic ingredients: Products that contain at least 70 to 94 percent organic ingredients are in another category. They can display the

Above: Vegetables at a Florida farmers market display the USDA certified organic seal. The farmers who grew these vegetables had to meet standards set by the NOP in order use this symbol with their produce.

" Protecting public health is more than filling out forms . . . it involves taking responsibility.

–GARRY MCKEE, ADMINISTRATOR OF THE USDA'S FOOD SAFETY AND INSPECTION SERVICE

USA TODAY · NOVEMBER 11, 2003

phrase "made with organic ingredients." They cannot, however, display the USDA organic seal.

If a product contains less than 70 percent organic ingredients, it cannot display the term *organic* anywhere on its packaging.

DISPUTES AND DEBATES

Debate erupted almost from the moment the standards were established. Organic producers and consumer watchdog organizations interpreted the law differently. They argued about enforcement of the regulations. Some claimed that a few large organic producers deliberately bent the rules. The Organic Consumers Association said the producers may have met the letter of the law. But, they added, these producers often intentionally got around the intent of the law.

The debate focused especially on the "access to pasture" regulation. That regulation required organic producers to provide cattle "access to the outdoors, shade, shelter, exercise areas, fresh air, and direct sunlight suitable to the species, its stage of production, the climate and the environment." Yet, critics claimed that some organic dairies had been permitted to sell milk as organic even though their cows did not have access to pasture.

Critics lobbied for stricter enforcement of the rules. Yet, according to Ronnie Cummins, national director of the Organic Consumers Association, the USDA's organic certification regulations provided many loopholes for companies. For example, the "access to pasture" regulations didn't specify the exact number of days a cow had to be allowed on pastureland. Consequently, it left room for producers to decide just how many days that should be.

Critics say the USDA was not interested in holding organic farmers to the letter of the law. They also believe that the USDA simply did not have the money to hire enough staff to do so. Some say, however, that the regulation was not specific enough. The NOP itself admitted that the vagueness of the law made it difficult to enforce.

All the same, according to organic producers, the intent of the law was clear. As far as Cummins was concerned, "Organic dairy means...you pasture the animals every single day of the growing season and means they are raised from birth organic. You can't buy cheap heifers [young cows that have not produced a calf] and bring them onto an organic farm and say they are organic."

Jim Riddle, chairman of the National Organic Standards Board, agreed. Riddle recommended the rules be revised. He wanted to make it "clear that organic milk can come only from cows that graze in pastures

> **"Organic dairy means ... you pasture the animals every single day of the growing season and means they are raised from birth organic. You can't buy cheap heifers and bring them onto an organic farm and say they are organic."**
>
> **–RONNIE CUMMINS,** NATIONAL DIRECTOR, ORGANIC CONSUMERS ASSOCIATION, 2008

during the growing season." As he put it, "There are certain dairies where ten months out of the year the cows are confined and fed out of a trough. Then two months of the year, when they're just about to give birth, they're in the pasture."

After years of wrangling, new regulations were finally adopted in 2010. Those regulations updated the pasture standards for organic livestock. Specifically, the new rules require that dairy cows and other ruminants must be let onto pasture during the grazing season. That season is at least 120 days per year. In addition, the rules prohibit continuous confinement of any animal in feedlots.

This new regulation has not ended the ongoing debate, however. Many smaller organic farmers and the larger operations like Aurora Dairy continue to disagree. Clark Driftmier, marketing director for the Aurora company, argues that the real issue is not access to pasture. Driftmier believes small organic farmers feel threatened by larger-scale producers, such as Aurora. Because of its larger size, Aurora can produce dairy products more cheaply. Since small farmers cannot limit the size of larger farms, says Driftmier, they look for other issues. For example, they accuse larger farms of not providing the required access to pasture. "The argument is really about scale," Driftmier says. "But it's being fought using pasture because it's generally acknowledged that scale is not a way to kick someone out of organic."

Aurora cofounder Retzloff is prepared to continue to fight those who accuse Aurora of not following organic regulations. "Organic stewardship [careful, responsible management] is one of our founding principles at Aurora Organic Dairy," he says. "And, personally, having worked so hard to create the organic standards and support the organic community throughout my career, makes organic stewardship part of my very being, my soul."

CHAPTER THREE

Is Organic Food Better for Your Health?

FROM THE TIME HE COULD WALK, JAMES ALWAYS seemed to be "on the go." As he got older, he had problems playing with other children. He constantly fought with his sister.

By the time James got to kindergarten, he couldn't sit still for even a short period of time. He found it difficult to pay attention or follow directions. "He often spent his four hours a day in class lying on the floor under the table," his mother remembers. He wandered "aimlessly through the classroom, touching everything, unable to stay on task no matter what he chose to do."

Finally, a psychologist provided the diagnosis. James suffered from a behavioral disorder called attention deficit hyperactivity disorder (ADHD). An

Left: Children gather apples at a pick-your-own farm. Many consumers are turning to organic produce because of concerns about the health risks associated with pesticide use in conventional farming.

estimated 8 to 10 percent of U.S. school-age children have ADHD.

Scientists and doctors are still not sure what causes the disorder. They suspect it is a combination of factors. These potential factors range widely from genetics to high levels of lead in paint from older buildings. ADHD might even be caused by secondhand cigarette smoke.

ANOTHER POSSIBLE CULPRIT

Recently, though, attention has focused on organophosphates-based pesticides. Organophosphates are used in nerve gas, a chemical weapon classified by the United Nations as a weapon of mass destruction. Organophosphates are also used in many insecticides and herbicides. They are found in trace amounts on commercially grown fruits and vegetables. These include strawberries, apples, peaches, celery, spinach, and potatoes. Once taken into the body, these pesticides break down into compounds that can be detected in human urine samples.

In 2010 a joint University of Montreal and Harvard University research study brought national attention to these chemicals. The study showed that children with higher levels of organophosphates in their urine were more likely to be diagnosed with ADHD.

Above: A woman selects conventionally grown apples from a grocery store bin. Small amounts of organophosphates, a component of many pesticides, are found on nonorganic apples.

Antipesticide groups cited the study as additional evidence that conventional agriculture is harmful. One such group is the Environmental Working Group. This is a nonprofit advocacy organization with the mission of creating awareness of the potential health hazards of toxic contaminants. The group announced: "The growing consensus among scientists is that small doses of pesticides and other chemicals can cause lasting damage to human health, especially during fetal development and early childhood."

Above: **A spraying machine applies pesticides to fruit trees in a Pennsylvania orchard. Conventional agriculturists state that such pesticides are both essential to their farming and safe for consumers.**

Conventional agriculture associations fought back. Hembree Brandon of the *Western Farm Press* wrote, "As if it weren't bad enough that farmers are accused of causing all manner of environmental ills," he wrote, "now the antipesticide contingent wants to make them responsible for kids having ADHD." Brandon noted that conventional agriculture provides the United States with "the most abundant and cheapest food on the planet."

Researchers who conducted the study pointed out that they did not find a direct link between organophosphates and ADHD. In addition, they noted that the study involved only 1,139 young people in the United States and Canada. It measured only one urine sample from each child. Yet, they maintained that there was a potential link between pesticide exposure and ADHD.

The debate about pesticides and ADHD is just one aspect of the debate over conventional farming practices versus organic agriculture.

Toxin study raises alarm about levels in kids' blood

From the Pages of
USA TODAY

A government report released Friday shows that human exposure to lead in the environment continues to decline, but it also identified higher-than-expected blood levels of other toxins in children.

The report by the Centers for Disease Control and Prevention [CDC] is the second federal study designed to measure human exposure to environmental toxins, pollutants and chemicals. The first report, issued last year, identified 27 chemicals in the human body. The new report tracked 116 chemicals in the blood and urine of 2,500 adults and children.

Another study released late last week by the Mount Sinai School of Medicine in New York found a total of 167 chemicals in nine volunteers, including 76 chemicals linked to cancer.

Such chemicals get into the human body when people eat food laced with pesticides or use personal-care products such as cosmetics. People also can inhale or pick up toxins and pollutants from the environment, says Jane Houlihan of the Washington-based Environmental Working Group, which collaborated on the Mount Sinai study.

Conventional agriculture typically uses a variety of chemical pesticides. Organic agriculture does not.

The debate focuses on three questions:

1. Are chemical pesticides harmful to a person's health?
2. Are they essential to meet global food needs?
3. Does food grown without chemical pesticides contain more and better nutrients?

ARE PESTICIDES HARMFUL?

Supporters of chemical pesticides dismiss concerns as overblown. They point out that the USDA must approve all pesticides. Every pesticide is

The chemicals have been linked to cancer and other diseases, but no one really knows the health effect when they are found in low levels.

Though the verdict is still out on the cause-and-effect relationship between low levels of chemicals in the body and health problems, some experts, such as Philip Landrigan, lead author of the Mount Sinai study, worry that even low levels could lead to diseases in some people. These chemicals are of particular concern for children, who often pick up more toxins from the environment, he says.

The CDC report identified higher-than-expected levels of an insecticide called chlorpyrifos in kids. Children had body levels of chlorpyrifos that were twice as high as adults, a finding that raised a red flag for environmental health expert Lynn Goldman of Johns Hopkins University in Baltimore. Chlorpyrifos has been linked to nervous system damage. Children get higher levels in their bodies because they play on the floor, where insecticides settle after being applied in the home, Goldman says.

The CDC also found that the percentage of children with elevated blood levels of lead had declined from 4.4% in its first report to 2.2% as measured in this report. Elevated lead exposure has been linked to lower IQ and other developmental problems.

–Kathleen Fackelmann

thoroughly tested to make sure it is effective and safe for the environment and consumers.

Still, most research shows that conventionally grown products have higher levels of pesticide residue than organic crops. Edward Groth III is a senior scientist at Consumers Union, publisher of *Consumer Reports* magazine. He puts it this way: "Consumers who buy organic fruits and vegetables are exposed to just one-third as many residues as they'd eat in conventionally grown foods."

Does it necessarily follow that crops with higher levels of pesticide residue are dangerous? Not according to the USDA, which states that the residue on conventional farming products

> " **The pesticide issue just scares me—it wigs me out to think about the amount of chemicals that might be going into my kid.** "

–EIN O'NEAL, PARENT

USA TODAY · NOVEMBER 2, 2005

is too small an amount to be dangerous to humans.

Biologist Alex Avery dismisses the concern over pesticides on food products. In his book, *The Truth about Organic Foods*, Avery says the amount of pesticides on food crops is miniscule. It is about the same as "one penny in $10 million, or one inch [2.5 centimeters] in 16,000 miles [25,750 kilometers]." In other words, it is not something to worry about.

Opponents of pesticides disagree. They believe pesticides can cause serious illnesses. These illnesses include damage to the central nervous system and even cancer. Antipesticide groups point out that food grown without hormones, antibiotics, pesticides, and synthetic fertilizers limits exposure to toxic chemicals. It stands to reason, they say, that such foods offer significant health benefits.

USA TODAY Snapshots®

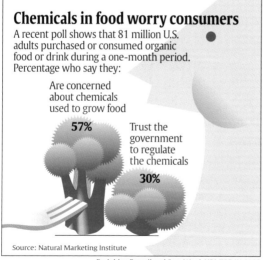

Chemicals in food worry consumers

A recent poll shows that 81 million U.S. adults purchased or consumed organic food or drink during a one-month period. Percentage who say they:

Are concerned about chemicals used to grow food
57%

Trust the government to regulate the chemicals
30%

Source: Natural Marketing Institute

By Ashley Burrell and Sam Ward, USA TODAY, 2005

An article in *Environmental Health Perspectives*, a journal published by the U.S. National Institute of Environmental Health Sciences, supports this view. The article argues that pesticides produce both short- and long-term effects on human health. "The long-term effects of pesticides include elevated cancer risks and disruption of the body's reproductive, immune, endocrine, and nervous systems."

A 2010 report by the President's Cancer Panel concurs. The report suggests that eating organically grown food helps reduce exposure to environmental chemicals that can increase the risk of cancer. Titled *Reducing Environmental Cancer Risk: What We Can Do Now*, the report stops short of recommending an organic diet. It does, however, encourage consumers to decrease their exposure to pesticides. Consumers should, when possible, choose "food grown without pesticides or chemical fertilizers and [should wash] conventionally grown produce to remove residues."

The report advises President Obama to do everything in his power to remove cancer-causing chemicals and "toxins from our food, water, and air." It says these contaminants "needlessly increase health care costs, cripple our nation's productivity, and devastate American lives."

CRITICAL FOR FOOD PRODUCTION?

Conventional agricultural advocates argue that from an economic standpoint, the use of pesticides is essential. Pesticides are critical to producing high-quality food at an economical price and in the quantity necessary to feed the world. Some say that without the use of pesticides, food production would drop by as much as 30 to 40 percent. In addition, food would be more expensive and of poorer quality. Others say the elimination of pesticides could lead to widespread global hunger. It would be impossible to provide enough fruits and vegetables to maintain a healthy population.

Above: Iowa corn on a conventional farm. Opponents debate whether organic agriculture can match the quantity of food produced using conventional methods.

Organic advocates say such claims are exaggerations. They maintain that organic agriculture can provide food just as efficiently as conventional farming.

BETTER NUTRITION?

Is food grown without the use of pesticides really better for you? Does it contain more and better nutrients? The jury is still out. That's mainly because different research groups have come to different conclusions after reviewing the studies. Some say organic food has no more nutritional value than food grown with the use of pesticides. Others say just the opposite. For example, in 2008 the Organic Center published a report claiming the "nutritional superiority" of plant-based organic food. The report was based on a review of ninety-seven studies. These studies compared the nutritional quality of organic and conventional foods.

Organic Tomatoes Better for Heart and Blood Pressure?

Organic tomatoes have significantly higher levels of flavonoids compared to nonorganic tomatoes. That's the conclusion of a ten-year study carried out by researchers at the University of California, Davis.

Flavonoids are a class of water-soluble pigments. They are present in many plants. Flavonoids are known to lower hypertension (high blood pressure). That, in turn, can help lower the risk of heart disease and stroke. Also, flavonoids may provide some protection from cancer and dementia.

In the study, researchers found that levels of flavonoids in organic tomatoes were 79 to 97 percent higher than in nonorganic tomatoes. The organic tomatoes were grown in soil without the addition of chemically synthesized fertilizers.

Above: Researchers found more healthy flavonoids in organic tomatoes than in nonorganic tomatoes.

Still, researchers say, there are thousands of flavonoids in the average person's diet. They suggest that a comprehensive investigation of these flavonoids is needed.

Charles Benbrook, chief scientist for the Organic Center, concluded that organic is, on average, 25 percent "more nutritious in terms of vitamins and minerals than products derived from industrial agriculture." Benbrook and his associates concluded that organic fruits, vegetables, and grains contain higher levels of eight of eleven nutrients studied.

Critics such as Joseph D. Rosen attacked these conclusions. Rosen is a retired professor of food toxicology at Rutgers University in New Jersey. He is also an adviser to the American Council on Science and Health (ACSH). The ACSH is a nonprofit consumer education association concerned with food, nutrition, chemicals, pharmaceuticals, the environment, and health. Rosen questioned the Organic Center's analysis of the data. He also pointed out that the center is supported by contributions from organic food companies. "The main interest of those companies is shareholder profits," Rosen says, "not improved consumer health."

Rosen examined the same data that the center had analyzed. But he reached different conclusions. He said that Benbrook's analysis included many errors. For example, Rosen found that conventional products were actually 2 percent more nutritious than organic food. Rosen says claims that organic food is more nutritious are not supported by the FDA or other government organizations.

A year after the report by the Organic Center, the *American Journal of Clinical Nutrition* published yet another review by a team of researchers. This team was headed by Alan Dangour. Dangour is a nutritionist for the London School of Hygiene and Tropical Medicine. Dangour's researchers analyzed fifty-five studies. Carried out over a fifty-year time span, these studies focused on the nutritional content of organic versus conventional crops. Twenty-three categories of nutrients were analyzed. Twenty categories showed no significant differences in nutrient content between organically grown and conventionally grown food products.

Yet, Dangour was cautious in drawing any conclusions. He stopped short of claiming that organically grown food was not nutritionally better: "We're not saying there's no difference [between the nutritional content of organically and conventionally grown foods;] we're saying there's no evidence [of any difference]." Dangour agriculture proponents took issue with Dangour's report. Calling it too narrow in scope, they also cited flaws in the methods of analysis.

And so the debate continues. Both sides would probably agree on one thing. More research is needed. In the meantime, the conclusion by the USDA sums up where the debate stands: "The verdict regarding the overall 'winner' [between organic produce and

> " We're not saying there's no difference [between the nutritional content of organically and conventionally grown foods] we're saying there's no evidence [of any difference]. "
>
> **–ALAN DANGOUR,** NUTRITIONIST FOR THE LONDON SCHOOL OF HYGIENE AND TROPICAL MEDICINE, 2009

believes additional high-quality field trials are needed. These trials should compare crops grown on the same land. Organic conventionally grown produce] in terms of nutritional superiority may not be known for some time."

CHAPTER FOUR

Pesticides and the Environment

IN 1962 AMERICAN MARINE BIOLOGIST AND NATURE writer Rachel Carson (1907–1964) published a controversial book called *Silent Spring*. The book's title described a future spring when no songbirds would be heard singing because they had all died from pesticide poisoning.

One of Carson's strongest arguments against the use of pesticides in agriculture was aimed at one particular pesticide—DDT. Farmers throughout the world had begun to rely on this powerful chemical during the second half of the twentieth century. There were several reasons for this. First, the chemical is toxic to a wide range of insects. Second, it is not water soluble. That means rain can't wash it away. Finally, DDT was and still is inexpensive and easy to apply.

Carson wrote that DDT and other pesticides were causing great harm to wildlife and waterways. Earth's ecosystem might eventually be destroyed unless

Left: Rachel Carson with her influential book *Silent Spring* in 1963. Carson's book led to a national ban on the use of the pesticide DDT in the United States.

Above: **A farmer sprays cattle with DDT in 1947 to rid them of flies, lice, and ticks. Before the publication of the book *Silent Spring*, DDT was used widely in the United States.**

something were done. Carson said the "rain of chemicals" had to be stopped. Carson also believed that pesticides were causing cancer and other illnesses in humans.

Many condemned Carson's book. They said no evidence supported the idea that DDT was harming the environment or that it increased the risk of cancer. They called Carson a "hysterical woman" and put down her "emotional arguments."

They said her concerns about pesticides had very little to do with scientific fact. Chemical manufacturing companies were particularly critical. "If man were to follow the teachings of Miss Carson, we would return to the Dark Ages," wrote a biochemist at American Cyanamid. "And the insects and diseases and vermin would once again inherit the earth."

But others supported Carson. They said *Silent Spring* offered a critical and scientifically based point of view on the state of the environment. U.S. Supreme Court justice William O. Douglas praised her work. He called the book "the most important chronicle of this century for the human race."

For ten years after the publication of *Silent Spring*, the debate over pesticides and the environment raged on. Then, in 1970, President Richard Nixon proposed the formation of the Environmental Protection Agency (EPA) to protect human health and the environment. A nationwide ban on DDT soon followed in 1972.

ANNIVERSARY DEBATE

Even in the twenty-first century, debate over *Silent Spring* continues. For example, the year 2007 was the one-hundredth anniversary of Carson's birth. Members of Congress from Maryland and Pennsylvania introduced a resolution to honor her. But Republican senator Tom Coburn of Oklahoma objected. Coburn, a doctor, put a hold on the bill, hoping to prevent its approval.

After an outpouring of public support for the bill, Coburn changed his mind. The Senate unanimously approved the bill. But Coburn's objection had been that Carson was responsible for millions of deaths around the world because of her "junk science." Many wondered what he meant.

According to Coburn and others, after the publication of Carson's book, many countries stopped spraying DDT to kill mosquitoes. Mosquitoes spread deadly diseases, such as malaria. The decision not to use DDT, says Coburn, led to the deaths of millions of people in Africa and other parts of the world from malaria and other mosquito-borne diseases. The World Health Organization (WHO) says that the use of DDT to fight malaria far outweighs any potential risks to human and environmental health. DDT proponent Angela Logomasini agrees. Logomasini is director of risk and environmental policy at the Competitive Enterprise Institute, a nonprofit public policy group.

November 29, 2000

Poor nations take lesser of two evils: DDT over malaria

From the Pages of USA TODAY

A coalition [group] of public health advocates is rallying on behalf of an unlikely cause: DDT, an environmental nemesis [enemy] they say is the most effective weapon ever found in the war against malaria.

The pesticide DDT was banned in the USA in 1972, after decades of use in agriculture, because of its harmful effects on fish and wildlife.

But the chemical is still being used elsewhere in the world to kill mosquitoes that transmit malaria, a disease that infects an estimated 300 million people a year, killing 2.5 million.

"If we just focus on the issue of controlling malaria, DDT is the closest to a miracle chemical that has ever come along," says Donald Roberts, a malaria expert with the Uniformed Services University of the Health Sciences in Bethesda, Md. "I am not convinced we have a chemical . . . that can match it."

Roberts is the U.S. spokesman for the Save Children From Malaria campaign, an international initiative aiming to persuade participants in a

Above: A worker in India sprays DDT in an effort to control malaria-bearing mosquitos.

meeting next week in Johannesburg, South Africa, to permit the use of DDT in countries where malaria persists.

Representatives from more than 120 countries are expected to finalize the language of a U.N. Environment Programme treaty that would phase out 12 chemicals considered "persistent organic pollutants," or POPs. They include DDT, chlordane, dioxin, and PCBs.

Clifton Curtis, director of the global toxics initiative for the World Wildlife Fund, one of the environmental groups leading the effort to phase out or ban the pollutants, says it is unlikely the treaty will bar DDT's anti-malarial uses.

"For each of the 12 POPs, countries are afforded the opportunity to say they need a country-specific exemption," he says. "In the case of DDT, a number of countries have requested an exemption for malaria use."

While DDT is likely to be banned for agricultural uses, he says, "for malaria control, it's clear that there is the need for continued use of DDT, and that use should be allowed until and unless effective alternatives are in place."

But Roger Bate of the Johannesburg-based group, Africa Fighting Malaria, says the treaty would put "onerous [difficult] reporting restrictions" on countries that use DDT. The restrictions, he says, would discourage the use of DDT by the overburdened public health systems in the poorest countries.

An analysis by the World Health Organization last year found 23 nations using DDT for malaria, Bate says, but "as of a month ago, only nine had asked for an exemption to use DDT. Colombia and Mexico have stockpiles of it, but for the other 12, it's just uncertain."

He says health officials in some countries, including Mozambique, one of the world's poorest nations, "have been put under pressure. They are concerned they will lose aid money if they use DDT."

Newer chemical alternatives are many times more expensive than DDT, Bate says. "India can only afford to spray 70% of malarious areas with DDT," he says. "If they use the next cheapest alternative, they can only spray 23%."

The fact that DDT persists in soil for long periods is "a double-edged sword," Roberts says, making it dangerous for use in agriculture but ideal for malaria control. It maintains its ability to repel mosquitoes after being sprayed once a year on walls inside homes.

–Anita Manning

In 2007 Logomasini wrote an opinion piece in the *Washington Post*. She wrote, "There is no compelling body of evidence that DDT causes any human health problems." She went on to explain that to control malaria, underdeveloped nations spray DDT only in and around homes. It is not sprayed widely enough to affect wildlife.

In 2002 Ronald Bailey, science editor for *Reason* magazine, summed up the opinion of many of Carson's critics: "Billions of dollars have been wasted chasing imaginary risks without measurably improving American health." Was Carson wrong about the effect of pesticides on the environment? To fully understand the debate about pesticides in the environment, it is important to first understand what pesticides are.

WHAT ARE PESTICIDES?

The term *pest* in agriculture refers to a wide range of organisms that may harm or slow the growth of crops or livestock. It includes weeds and insects—such as cockroaches and mosquitoes. It also refers to fungi, bacteria, and viruses that cause plant diseases. The EPA defines a pesticide as any "chemical used to prevent, destroy, or repel pests."

Every year, U.S. farmers alone apply an estimated one billion pounds (454 million kilograms) of pesticides to control pests that destroy food crops. Yet, even with the widespread use of pesticides, scientists estimate that as much as one-third of the world's food crop is destroyed each year by pests.

The use of pesticides in agriculture is not new. Inorganic pesticides, such as sulfur and arsenic, have been used for thousands of years. The Sumerians—an early civilization in southern Mesopotamia (modern-day Iraq) more than five thousand years ago—used sulfur to control pests. The ancient Greeks and Romans also used sulfur, as well as oil and other materials, to protect their crops from pests.

By the 1940s, modern manufacturers were producing

synthetic pesticides, such as DDT. DDT is made from highly toxic organochlorine chemical compounds. Modern pesticides generally can be divided into three main groups. They include herbicides, insecticides, and fungicides. These groups are organized according to the specific purpose of the pesticide.

Herbicides form the largest group of pesticides that farmers use throughout the world. Herbicides destroy or control a wide variety of weeds and other unwanted plants. Farmers on nearly all the agricultural land in the United States currently treat their crops with some type of herbicide.

Insecticides make up the second-largest group of pesticides.

This category is divided into four major chemical classifications, including organochlorines (of which DDT is one) and organophosphates. The organophosphates include malathion. That's the most commonly used insecticide in the United States. (In 2010 the EPA restricted the use of malathion near salmon streams because it negatively affects the behavior of certain endangered salmon.)

Fungicides are chemicals used mainly to protect agricultural crops and seeds from various fungi, such as mold, mildew, and rust. Some fungicides prevent or slow the growth of fungi. Other fungicides kill the disease after it appears on or near the plant.

66 Many people are making a statement when they buy organic food that they care about the environment and want to promote sustainable agriculture. 99

–LAURA COBLENTZ, HORIZON ORGANIC DAIRY,
USA TODAY · OCTOBER 15, 2002

Valley of plenty — and worry

Calif.

California's Central Valley is the most productive agricultural region in the nation. It's also a rapidly growing residential area. The combination of an expanding population living alongside farming's toxic pesticides is raising concern.

Sacramento

Westley

Central Valley

Bakersfield

The Central Valley produces more than half of California's agricultural goods. If it were a state, the area would have the largest agricultural income in the USA.

The valley's agricultural richness and diversity feed the pesticide problem. Major crops and farm products include:
▶**Livestock:** Cattle, dairy, chickens
▶**Fruits:** Grapes, tomatoes, cherries, peaches
▶**Field crops:** Alfalfa, cotton
▶**Nuts:** Almonds, walnuts, pistachios
▶**Other:** Carrots, potatoes

A sample of pesticides used in the Central Valley
Fumigants
▶Used in production of fruits, vegetables and nuts
▶Health hazards include birth defects, prostate cancer and brittle bones
▶Examples: Methyl bromide, sulfuryl fluoride

Insecticides
▶Used on fruits, vegetables and nuts
▶Health hazards include cancer and neurological damage
▶Examples: Malathion, diazinon, chlorpyrifos

Herbicides
▶Used on grapes, citrus, corn, soybeans and nuts
▶Health hazards include cancer, miscarriages and sterility
▶Examples: Atrazine, simazine, paraquat

Source: California Agricultural Statistics Service and Pesticide Action Network North America

USA TODAY, 2005

Two other classes of pesticides include rodenticides to control rodents and antimicrobials to control bacteria.

ADVANTAGES OF PESTICIDES

Since their development, synthetic pesticides have helped to increase crop production. They have also reduced insectborne diseases. According to some estimates, even with pesticides, at least 13 percent of all U.S. crops are lost to insects. Without pesticides, some believe that this percentage would skyrocket. As a result, the cost of food would increase dramatically.

One of the biggest advantages of pesticides is their

cost-effectiveness. Pesticide companies estimate that for every dollar farmers spend on pesticides, they make a profit of up to five dollars on crops saved from pests. Furthermore, because so many pesticides are available, farmers can target specific pests with the most effective pesticide.

Much of the savings comes from reduced labor costs. Without pesticides, farmers must hire additional workers to weed and control pests by hand. For example, late blight is a notorious fungal disease that attacks potatoes and tomatoes. It causes millions of dollars in losses for farmers each year. Fungicides help protect tomato plants and potato plants from late blight. But for farmers who don't use fungicides, the only way to protect against the fungus is to remove and destroy infected plants. This requires additional labor, which has to be done by hand.

Proponents of pesticides point out that before a pesticide is approved for use, the EPA does a wide range of environmental, laboratory, and field studies. These test the toxicity of the pesticide. They also look to see what happens to that pesticide in the soil, air, and water. Proponents see huge advancements in pesticides over the years. For example, pesticides are less toxic yet more powerful

Above: Potatoes infected with late blight, like this one, are shrunken on the outside and rotted on the inside. Fungicides control this disease.

than in the past. As a result, farmers require fewer chemicals to achieve the same results in their fields.

DISADVANTAGES OF PESTICIDES

Critics of pesticides say the disadvantages of the chemicals far outweigh their advantages. The U.S. Geological Survey, for example, states that pesticides "raise questions about possible adverse [harmful] effects on the environment, including water quality."

Critics also say that pesticide sprays are not as economical as proponents suggest. Only 1 to 2 percent of the chemicals actually reach their intended targets. The other 98 percent ends up in the air, surface water, groundwater, wildlife, and even humans.

In addition, while killing unwanted or harmful insects, pesticides also kill beneficial insects. These helpful insects feed on insects that are harmful to crops. For example, whiteflies are tiny, snow-white insects that farmers often describe as "flying dandruff." They destroy cotton, melons, and other crops in the Southwest. One enemy of the whitefly is the lady beetle. Lady beetles naturally feed on the whiteflies in crop fields.

Pesticides designed to kill whiteflies also kill the lady beetles, however. As a result, farmers often see more whiteflies in their fields after applying pesticides. What is more, whiteflies seem to quickly build up immunity (resistance) to pesticides. This makes it necessary to use stronger, more toxic chemicals to get rid of them. Some scientists suggest this is a common problem with pesticides, one that adds to their potential danger to the environment and to human health.

Opponents of pesticides object to the theory that without pesticides, farmers would not be able to produce enough food to feed the world. They maintain that we already produce more than enough grain to feed the world. According to the National Sustainable Agriculture Information Service, "The amount of grain produced in the world in 1999 could, by

Above: Whiteflies, shown here on a leaf, destroy cotton, melons, and other crops. Conventional farmers use pesticides to kill these bugs.

But citizens didn't have enough money to buy the food, so they starved.

Opponents of pesticides also question the reliability of EPA testing of these chemicals. The EPA states that "because they are designed to kill or otherwise adversely [negatively] affect living organisms, pesticides may pose some risk to humans, animals, or the environment." The effects of pesticides remain in the environment for years after they are used. For example, though banned in 1972, organochlorine, an organic compound in DDT, is still in the environment. In 2010 the U.S. Geological Survey measured the amount of organochlorine in sediment (rock, sand, and minerals that settle to the bottom of bodies of water) and in fish tissue samples. The study found levels that were higher than is safe for freshwater life and the wildlife that preys on fish.

itself, sustain 8 billion people—two billion more than our current world population." The real problem, they say, is distribution of food. For example, during the Irish potato famine in the mid-1800s or the famine in Bangladesh in 1974 plenty of potatoes and grain, respectively, were available in warehouses.

Pesticides and the American Bald Eagle

In 1782, when the bald eagle was declared the national emblem of the United States, the U.S. population of this majestic bird was more than 300,000. Two hundred years later, fewer than 450 bald eagles remained. The U.S. government officially declared the bald eagle an endangered species. The bird joined other animals on the Federal List of Endangered and Threatened Wildlife and Plants.

What happened? The near loss of the bald eagle had many causes. In 1984 the National Wildlife Federation listed the leading causes of eagle deaths: hunting, electrocution as a result of flying into power lines, and collisions in flight. Another reason for the dramatic reduction in the population of the bald eagle had to do with the pesticide DDT.

Until 1972 many U.S. farmers used DDT to protect their crops. Often rain would wash the pesticide into rivers and streams, where it poisoned fish. The bald eagle would, in turn, eat the fish. While the DDT didn't affect the eagle directly, it affected the bird's calcium metabolism. This led to eagles laying eggs with very thin shells. The nesting mother would usually unintentionally crush the eggs with the weight of her body before they could hatch.

In 1972 the U.S. government banned DDT throughout the United States. By 2007 the bald eagle population had made a remarkable recovery. In that year, the United States had an estimated ten thousand nesting pairs of bald eagles, and the bird was taken off the endangered species list. Many people believe the bald eagle was saved from extinction by the removal of DDT from the environment.

ALTERNATIVES AND SAFER PESTICIDES

Opponents of pesticides recognize the importance of controlling pests. But they say farmers can use other methods, such as crop rotation. This involves planting a different crop each year in a particular field. Pests and weeds tend to take over a plot of land if the same crop is planted there year after year. A new crop interferes with the life cycle of pests

Rachel Carson receives credit for eliminating DDT in the United States. However, Carson never advocated for a total ban on the pesticide. Rather, she argued for a more responsible use of DDT—and of all pesticides. Have we achieved that goal? John Quiggin and Tim Lambert, university professors in Australia, think so. As they wrote in 2008, "Modern uses of insecticides are far closer

> **" Modern uses of insecticides are far closer to the methods advocated by [Rachel] Carson [author of *Silent Spring*] than to the practices she criticized. "**
>
> **–JOHN QUIGGIN,** ECONOMIST AT THE UNIVERSITY OF QUEENSLAND, AUSTRALIA, AND TIM LAMBERT, COMPUTER SCIENTIST AT THE UNIVERSITY OF NEW SOUTH WALES, AUSTRALIA, 2008

that prefer the original crop. A second alternative is to plant trap crops. These are specific plants that attract pests away from the main crop. Farmers can also rely on companion planting. This means planting insect-repelling plants next to crops that need protection from certain pests.

to the methods advocated by Carson than to the practices she criticized." Until more cost-effective methods are developed, pesticides will undoubtedly continue to be the most widely used defense against agricultural pests throughout the world.

CHAPTER FIVE

Livestock and the Debate about CAFOs

NICK HUNT IS LIKE MANY MODERN-DAY RANCHERS. He understands the importance of good stewardship of the land. Hunt and his wife, Sue, are both fourth-generation farmers. They own and manage Clan Farms, a 2,400-acre (971-hectare) ranch in Atlantic, Iowa. Nick's great grandfather bought this land along the East Nishnabotna River more than one hundred years ago. Together with four employees, the Hunts farm 1,100 acres (445 hectares) of corn, 800 acres (324 hectares) of soybeans, and 200 acres (81 hectares) of alfalfa.

They also manage two feedlot operations. A feedlot (or feed yard) is a place where livestock are fattened before being moved to a processing facility. Large feedlots are called Concentrated Animal Feeding Operations (CAFOs). They are places where large numbers of livestock—including cattle, poultry, and swine—are raised

Left: Chickens are packed tightly into this Concentrated Animal Feeding Operation (CAFO) facility. The poultry will be fattened here before being moved to a processing plant.

in enclosed areas. These places don't have natural pastures or rangeland. The enclosed feedlot has no grass or other vegetation.

In the typical cycle of raising beef cattle, the animals spend most of their lives grazing on rangeland. Between the ages of twelve and sixteen months, they reach a weight of about 650 pounds (295 kg). Ranchers then transfer the cattle to a feedlot. They remain there for another three or four months before going to a processor. There, the animals are butchered for food and other products. For many critics, the CAFO is where problems begin.

THE DEBATE OVER CAFOs

CAFOs, such as those that Nick Hunt and his family manage, produce most of the meat, dairy, and poultry eaten in the United States. They are hotly debated among organic livestock farmers and conventional ranchers. Many citizens are also concerned about CAFOs.

Opponents of CAFOs often refer to these facilities as "factory farms." They claim that people who run CAFOs don't worry about human health or environmental issues or the ethical treatment of the animals.

One organization, Sustainable Table, is particularly opposed to CAFOs. Sustainable Table was organized in 2003. Its purpose is to help educate consumers about the U.S. agricultural system in the twenty-first century. The organization is particularly interested in how meat and dairy products are produced. According to Sustainable Table, "The concentration of hundreds or thousands of animals in a confined feedlot facility drastically reduces the welfare of these animals." CAFOs are said to create health risks for the animals and feedlot workers. They also reportedly produce large amounts of animal waste, which pollutes the environment. In general, many critics feel that all too often those who operate CAFOs are more concerned with profit than animal welfare.

Yet, owners of CAFOs say their concern with profit is exactly why they are also concerned about the well-being of their animals. Janet Riley is a spokeswoman for the American Meat Institute. She says there is no reason why the industry would want to mistreat animals. "Livestock are our raw materials," she says, "and hurting them makes as much sense as Detroit auto workers putting dents in the cars they make."

Nevertheless, many organizations reject the notion that CAFOs are as beneficial as proponents claim. The Humane Farming Association is one of the largest and most effective farm animal protection organizations in the country. As this association sees it, "The real costs of factory farming—in terms of the loss of family farms, food-borne illness, damage to the environment, and animal suffering—have been tremendous."

ETHICAL TREATMENT OF ANIMALS

Critics of CAFOs state that the feedlots crowd hundreds or, in the case of poultry, thousands of animals into cramped indoor facilities. This crowding limits the normal behavior and movement of animals. As a result, these animals have a greater potential for disease or injury. According to an independent report, conditions in many facilities are so harsh that they lead to undue suffering throughout much of an animal's life.

At some CAFO poultry farms, for example, chickens are kept in such tight quarters that they are unable to flap their

> **" Livestock are our raw materials and hurting them makes as much sense as Detroit auto workers putting dents in the cars they make. "**
>
> –JANET RILEY, AMERICAN MEAT INSTITUTE SPOKESPERSON, 1998

wings. They often become aggressive. To prevent aggressive behavior, factory farms often "debeak" their chickens. (They cut off the beaks.) Animal rights activists believe this is an extremely painful procedure.

Pigs are often confined in pens with concrete floors. This keeps them from their natural activity of rooting, or digging in the dirt. According to some reports, concrete floors cause deformities of the feet of pigs. Further, opponents of CAFOs claim many of these facilities feed cattle a grain-based diet. While this is inexpensive feed, it is also difficult for the animals to digest. Such a diet reportedly also reduces the nutritional value of the meat we get from the animals.

Above: These turkey hens have been debeaked to prevent aggressive behavior at a factory farm.

CAFOs AND THE ENVIRONMENT

Environmentalists are also concerned about CAFOs. This is because the confined animals create large amounts of waste. Some reports estimate that farm animal waste in the United States is more than 130 times greater than that produced by the human population.

Environmentalists believe that CAFO animal waste has many harmful consequences. In open pastures and rangeland, manure is spread out over a large area. The nutrients in the manure are recycled back into the soil. In CAFOs, however, the waste accumulates where the animals live. Eventually, farmers and ranchers collect the waste and spray it onto farm fields as fertilizer. According to the EPA, "The concentration of the wastes from these animals [in CAFOs] increases the potential to impact air, water, and land quality."

Studies suggest that factory farms are responsible for the release of more than 18 percent of greenhouse gas emissions worldwide. These gases result from the decomposition (breakdown) of manure. This process releases carbon dioxide, methane, and nitrous oxides into the atmosphere. These gases contribute to global warming by absorbing the sun's radiation and trapping its heat in Earth's atmosphere.

Finally, there is ongoing concern among environmentalists about millions of gallons of liquid waste contaminants, known as slurry. This liquid waste accumulates either in pits underneath the CAFO buildings or in nearby open-air pits or lagoons. The waste can leach (seep) into public water sources. Contaminated water can cause many human illnesses, for example, dysentery, cholera, diarrhea, and typhoid fever. The Centers for Disease Control and Prevention (CDC), based in Atlanta, Georgia, conducted a study of waterborne disease outbreaks. They concluded that in every case,

Above: A woman takes water samples to monitor a CAFO. The samples will be tested for contamination.

the cause could be traced back to livestock waste.

The U.S. government has tried to regulate CAFOs in order to protect the environment. Since 1972 the Federal Clean Water Act has governed water quality in the United States. Regulations require feedlots to prevent livestock waste run-off from reaching rivers and streams. This is because live-stock manure contains the nutrients phosphorous and nitrogen. These nutrients can contaminate drinking water, kill fish, and spread disease. Yet critics claim these regulations are rarely enforced.

CAFOs AND HEALTH

Many critics of CAFOs also say that the concentration of hun-dreds or thousands of animals in a confined feedlot facility creates health risks for both animals and humans. One risk comes from the poisonous gases that excessive manure releases into the air. In a University of Minnesota study, researchers found pneumonia-like lesions on the lungs of 65 percent of the thirty-four thousand hogs they inspected in CAFOs.

These gases can also be harmful to humans. In one study, 25 percent of workers in CAFOs had chronic bronchitis and nonallergic asthma. In a study at the University of Iowa, children living on corporate hog farms were twice as likely to develop asthma as children liv-ing on other farms. Some work-ers have even died from expo-sure to the toxic fumes.

CAFOs AND ANTIBIOTICS

In CAFOs, antibiotics are used for a number of reasons. They are widely used to treat dis-ease in livestock. They are also used to help prevent the spread of disease from one animal to others in the group. They are used to make animals grow more rapidly and produce more meat. Finally, they are used dur-ing high-risk periods for the animals. For example, during transport, animals often expe-rience stress, which can lead to disease.

Farmers give about 25 mil-lion pounds (11 million kg) of

> ❝ **The life of an animal in a factory farm is characterized by acute deprivation, stress, and disease.** ❞
>
> **–THE HUMANE FARMING ASSOCIATION,** 2011

antibiotics to animals each year. That's about half of all antibiotics produced annually in the United States. Such massive use of antibiotics gives bacteria the opportunity to mutate and to develop resistances to major antibiotics such as penicillin or tetracycline. In fact, some of these common antibiotics are no longer effective. Antibiotic-resistant bacteria can then infect humans, either through the consumption, handling, or processing of meat. The U.S. Government Accounting Office (GAO), known as the congressional watchdog, reports that the overuse of antibiotics in animals poses significant risk for humans.

THE OTHER SIDE

The United States has more than eight hundred thousand beef producers. These producers say they follow sound production practices. They produce safe, wholesome beef for consumers around the world. These practices are outlined in a 1996 document titled "Producer Code of Cattle Care." Some guidelines include

- providing adequate food, water, and care to protect livestock health and well-being;
- following disease prevention practices to protect each animal's health;
- providing facilities that allow safe and humane movement and/or restraint of livestock; and
- training personnel to properly handle and care for livestock.

"Growing concern" over marketing tainted beef

<u>From the Pages of</u>
USA TODAY

Beef containing harmful pesticides, veterinary antibiotics and heavy metals is being sold to the public because federal agencies have failed to set limits for the contaminants or adequately test for them, a federal audit [formal examination] finds.

A program set up to test beef for chemical residues [the remains of pesticides, veterinary antibiotics, or heavy metals such as copper and zinc used by the beef industry] "is not accomplishing its mission of monitoring the food supply for . . . dangerous substances, which has resulted in meat with these substances being distributed in commerce," says the audit by the U.S. Department of Agriculture's Office of Inspector General.

The health effects on people who eat such meat are a "growing concern," the audit adds.

The testing program for cattle is run by the USDA's Food Safety and Inspection Service (FSIS), which also tests meat for such pathogens [disease-carrying agents] as salmonella and certain dangerous strains of *E. coli*. The residue program [program to test for chemical residue] relies on assistance from the Environmental Protection Agency [EPA], which sets tolerance levels for human exposure to pesticides and other pollutants, and the Food and Drug Administration [FDA], which does the same for antibiotics and other medicines.

Limits have not been set by the EPA and FDA "for many potentially harmful substances, which can impair FSIS' enforcement activities," the audit found.

The FSIS said in a written statement that the agency has agreed with the inspector general on "corrective actions" and will work with the FDA and EPA "to prevent residues or contaminants from entering into commerce."

Even when the inspection service does identify a lot of beef with high levels of pesticide or antibiotics, it often is powerless to stop the distribution of that meat because there is no legal limit for those contaminants.

In 2008, for example, Mexican authorities rejected a U.S. beef shipment because its copper levels exceeded Mexican standards, the audit says. But because there is no U.S. limit, the FSIS had no grounds for blocking the beef's producer from reselling the rejected meat in the United States.

"It's unacceptable. These are substances that can have a real impact on public health," says Tony Corbo, a lobbyist for Food and Water Watch, a public interest group. "This administration is making a big deal about promoting exports, and you have Mexico rejecting our beef because of excessive residue levels. It's pretty embarrassing."

Above: Harmful substances such as the heavy metal copper, shown here, have been found in U.S. beef.

Some contamination is inadvertent [unintentional], such as pesticide residues in cows that drink water fouled by crop runoff. Other contaminants, such as antibiotics, often are linked to the use of those chemicals in farming. For example, the audit says, veal calves often have higher levels of antibiotic residue because ranchers feed them milk from cows treated with the drugs. Overuse of the antibiotics help create antibiotic-resistant strains of diseases.

The National Cattlemen's Beef Association declined to comment because officials there had not seen the audit.

The audit "shows clearly the need for quick action by Congress to place some reasonable limits on the use of antibiotics in farm animals," says Rep. Louise Slaughter, D-N.Y., who has more than 100 co-sponsors on her bill to ban seven types of antibiotics from being used indiscriminately [without oversight] in animal feed. "If we don't remedy this problem, who knows what kind of havoc these residues will have on our bodies."

–Peter Eisler

Above: Conventionally raised beef cattle feed on corn byproducts in the winter.

USA TODAY Snapshots®

Nothing to cluck at

Americans' per-capita consumption of meats and poultry in 2008:

(in pounds)

104.3

63

48.7

1   0.5

Poultry   Beef   Pork   Lamb   Veal

Source: U.S. Department of Agriculture, February 2009

By Anne R. Carey and Suzy Parker, USA TODAY, 2009

The beef producers' goal is to make sure that the animals are raised in a safe, healthy environment. That includes providing a nutritionally balanced and energy-rich diet. According to the Beef Cattlemen's Association, cattle can get the nutrients they need from eating a wide range of plants and grasses, including a variety of grains, such as corn. They point out that cattle in a feedlot are fed a combination of grain and hay. Their feed is formulated by professional nutritionists to make sure the animals get a well-balanced diet. Since grass doesn't grow year-round in most of the United States, feeding grains such as corn to cattle is necessary.

ANIMAL WELFARE

Managers of CAFOs argue that the public does not understand feedlot operations. They say that cattle have plenty of room to move around in feedlots. The cattle often crowd closely together on their own, which is their natural behavior. Some poultry scientists maintain that the objection to debeaking is based on emotions. They believe that debeaking is no more painful for chickens than clipping a fingernail is for humans.

CAFO managers also say that their facilities are not dirty. Rather, housing facilities are environmentally controlled. This helps to protect livestock from disease. According to Growing Indiana Agriculture (GINA), an industry education and awareness program, "Sheltered animals live a less stressful, healthier life than livestock that live outside, where they are constantly exposed to weather and predators."

USE OF ANTIBIOTICS

Some researchers believe farmers should limit the use of antibiotics that promote growth. Others think that such restrictions would increase the cost of producing animals. The result might be to increase the cost of animal products. One study suggests that the elimination of antibiotics in swine production alone would increase the cost to consumers by $700 million a year.

Industry proponents also point out that all animal antibiotics have gone through a strict testing process before the FDA approves them. In addition, strict guidelines are in place guiding the amount of time that must pass between when an animal receives an antibiotic and when the animal can safely enter the food supply. This is to make sure the antibiotic has cleared the animal's system before the animal is butchered for food.

The National Cattlemen's Association argues against the GAO's position that "the use of antibiotics in animals poses significant risks for human health." The industry group instead states that "multiple studies have reviewed whether antibiotic use in cattle production causes an increased risk to consumers . . . and none have found a connection."

HUMAN HEALTH AND THE ENVIRONMENT

In 1993 more than 700 people in four western states became violently ill after eating hamburger at various restaurants of one fast-food chain. More than 195 people were hospitalized, and four children died. The CDC issued an immediate recall of the contaminated hamburger meat.

CDC researchers soon discovered that all the illnesses were caused by a dangerous type of *E. coli* (*Escherichia coli*) bacteria. Critics of CAFOs claim feedlots promote *E. coli* because of dirty and confined living conditions. Yet, according to the National Beef Council, no valid research supports such claims. In fact, the Beef

USA TODAY Snapshots®

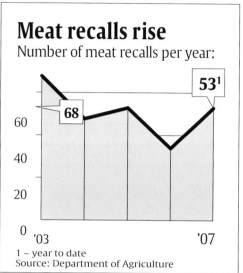

Meat recalls rise

Number of meat recalls per year:

68

53[1]

60

40

20

0

'03   '07

1 – year to date
Source: Department of Agriculture

By Marcy E. Mullins, USA TODAY, 2007

Above: In 1993 the CDC recalled hamburger meat contaminated with the dangerous *E. coli* bacteria.

Council states that the likelihood for cattle to carry *E. coli* is the same among cattle raised in pastures and cattle in feedlots. Furthermore, according to the CDC, the incidence of *E. coli* (and other foodborne illnesses) decreased by 25 percent between 1996 and 2004. During that period, the number of CAFOs actually increased.

With regard to the environment, conventional cattle ranchers maintain that since 2002 animal waste has been highly regulated by federal law. CAFOs that discharge waste into streams, rivers, or lakes must apply for a permit for their waste and follow strict regulations. The bottom line, according to the Cattlemen's Beef Board, is that all beef producers go to great lengths to be good stewards of the environment. They also provide the best care for livestock. "We take our responsibility to our cattle very seriously, and we believe even one instance of mistreatment is too many."

Nick Hunt agrees that good stewardship is important not only for the environment and for economic growth. It is also essential for future generations. "We want to pass the land on in the best shape—make it better, actually, than when we received the land."

> 66 **[The beef] industry says everything's perfect [with regard to the lives of farm animals] and the animal rights people say it's all bad, and the truth is in the middle. But I'm glad to say I'm seeing huge changes.** 99
>
> –TEMPLE GRANDIN, DESIGNER OF LIVESTOCK-HANDLING FACILITIES AND PROFESSOR OF ANIMAL SCIENCE AT COLORADO STATE UNIVERSITY
>
> USA TODAY · APRIL 13, 2003

CHAPTER SIX

Genetically Modified Food

FOR YEARS, CORN FARMER TIM HUME DEALT WITH A variety of pests in a traditional way. Several times throughout the growing season, he sprayed his crop with pesticides.

But in 1999, Hume decided to plant a new kind of crop, called *Bt* corn. This is a type of corn that kills invading insects with a sort of built-in pesticide. *Bt* corn is an example of a genetically modified crop. That means agricultural scientists have changed, or modified, its genes. Genetically modified crops are termed GM crops.

Bt is short for *Bacillus thuringiensis.* That's a naturally occurring bacterium found in soil throughout the world. The *Bt* bacterium produces proteins that are toxic to specific groups of insects. These include the European corn borer, the insect most damaging to corn throughout the United States. Corn borers cost farmers more than one billion dollars each year in lost crops.

Left: Researchers study genetically modified (GM) corn. To create GM crops, scientists modify the plants' genes. One goal of planting GM crops might be to create a pest-resistant crop.

When insects eat corn with *Bt* proteins, their own digestive systems activate the toxic form of the protein. This toxin causes the insect to die within two or three days. In 1996 scientists took a gene from the *Bt* bacterium and combined it with corn. The result was the GM corn. In the twenty-first century, farmers throughout the world plant *Bt* corn. In addition, many other GM crops have been developed and approved for planting and consumption worldwide. These crops include soybeans that can resist herbicides used to kill unwanted weeds. Other GM crops include GM sugar beets, squash, and papaya that are resistant to insects or viruses. In Hawaii, genetic modification produced papaya that resist ring spot virus. At one time, this virus threatened to destroy the huge papaya industry in that state.

While *Bt* corn seeds cost more, they do have advantages. For one, corn farmers spend less time looking for insects. They also don't need to spend as much money on pesticides. In addition, the *Bt* plant produces a greater yield.

GM crops were first introduced in the United States in 1996. Since then, GM crops have rapidly increased in number. In the twenty-first century, farmers in the United States plant 350 million acres (142 million hectares) of land for crops each year. More than 25 percent (nearly 90 million acres, or 36 million hectares) has been devoted to genetically engineered crops. What's even more amazing is that 70 to 80 percent of processed foods sold in supermarkets contain ingredients from genetically modified corn, soybeans, or cottonseed oil. Among many others, these processed foods include potato chips and other fried snack foods.

According to one report, economic and environmental factors explain the dramatic increase in GM crops. These include lower production costs, fewer pest problems, and better crop yields.

Yet, not everyone is happy about genetically modified crops or the foods they produce.

Above: The results of desertification (a process in which fertile land becomes desert) are shown here on the edge of China's Gobi Desert. Every year farmers lose fertile land to the neighboring deserts.

Critics often refer to them as Frankenfoods, after the fictional man-made monster, Frankenstein.

Ronnie Cummins, director of the Organic Consumers Association, says it is still too early to know the ultimate impact of GM food on humans. But he worries about it. According to Cummins, the younger generation "can look forward to a long-term epidemic of cancer, food allergies, sterility, learning disabilities, and birth defects."

Other people, however, disagree with this pessimistic outlook. They maintain that GM food is not only safe but is essential in providing enough food to feed the world in the future.

Globally, an estimated eight hundred million people do not have enough food to eat. By 2030 the global population is expected to reach eight billion people. Yet, the amount of available land for agriculture is limited. Only 10 percent of the world's land surface is suitable for farming. Some of that land is already experiencing problems from over-farming and soil erosion.

Terry Etherton, head of the Department of Dairy and Animal Science at Penn State University's College of Agricultural Sciences in Pennsylvania, is concerned about meeting the future food needs of the world. According to Etherton, "It's been estimated that the supply of food required to adequately meet human nutritional needs over the next forty years is equal to the amount of food previously produced throughout the entire history of humankind." Etherton claims that all the suitable and available land for agriculture is already being used. There is no more. The only answer to the world's food crisis, therefore, is genetically modified food.

AGRICULTURAL BIOTECHNOLOGY

All organisms (living beings) carry a genetic code. That code is made up of many sets of chemical instructions that make every living thing unique. In humans, for example, a person's genetic code determines whether he or she has blue eyes or brown eyes, among many other traits.

A GMO (genetically modified organism), or GEO (genetically engineered organism), is an organism that has been changed genetically. In agricultural biotechnology, this is a complicated process. Scientists start with genes from one species of plant or animal. They then insert those genes into another plant or animal. There, the inserted genes replicate, or copy, themselves. Using genetic engineering, scientists can pinpoint beneficial traits in plants or animals. Some of these beneficial traits could include better nutritional value. Other traits might include better flavor or a greater ability to fight pests or diseases. Scientists can insert these genes into other plants or animals. For example, the gene from a wild potato that is resistant to blight might be transferred to a potato crop that is grown for human consumption.

Biotechnology is not new. Farmers have crossbred plants

since the beginning of agricultural history. Their goal was to improve the yield of crop plants or to develop plants with greater resistance to pests or disease. They did this by selecting the seeds of the strongest crops for sowing the next planting season. They also combine different species organisms in a process known as hybridization. What is new are the extremely effective technological tools used for genetic modification in the twenty-first century.

The federal Food and Drug Administration has approved many GM crops. But as of 2010, it has not approved any GM cattle or poultry for food. Also, GM animals used for research purposes must be disposed of according to strict guidelines.

Their remains may not enter the food supply. Nevertheless, most scientists working in the field expect GM meat will be approved in the future.

In addition to GM crops, scientists are also attempting to develop GE cattle. For example, some scientists are working to develop cattle that are resistant to bovine spongiform encephalopathy, otherwise known as mad cow disease. This is a fatal disease of cattle that causes progressive damage to the sick animal's brain. Other scientists are trying to produce cattle that have fewer pollutants in their wastes. Scientists are also trying to improve the fat composition of cattle to include higher levels of nutritionally important omega-3 fatty acids.

"Under severe drought conditions we were able to see 20% yield improvement with those plants with the drought gene."

–ROBERT FRALEY, MONSANTO
USA TODAY · MARCH 17, 2010

BENEFITS OF GM FOODS

According to some scientists, agricultural biotechnology offers many benefits. First, more food can be produced using fewer pesticides and herbicides. That means crops are less expensive to grow. In addition, GM crops can be developed to better tolerate cold temperatures or extended droughts. These and other traits also make it possible to farm land that is currently not capable of producing crops.

Recently, USA TODAY reported that farmers in North and South America are increasingly using GM crops. These farmers say GM crops "protect the environment by decreasing pesticide use and making no-till crops [where the soil is not plowed] possible. This increases water retention and decreases erosion, and at least by some measures reduces carbon released into the atmosphere." But more important, according to some researchers, genetically modified crops can have an important impact on what is called "functional food." This is food that can help improve a person's health.

For example, in poor countries, many people don't get enough vitamin A. A lack of vitamin A can cause blindness and a weakened immune system. More than two million children die each year because of vitamin A shortages. At least five hundred thousand more children and adults become permanently blind. To find a solution to this health crisis, plant geneticists have developed a special type of rice, called golden rice. Golden rice produces a high level of beta-carotene, which is high in vitamin A. According to some scientists, golden rice has the potential to prevent, or at least to dramatically reduce, vitamin A deficiency among millions of people.

Hassan Adamu is a business man and former Nigerian minister of agriculture and rural development. In Nigeria, and throughout Africa, much of the population suffers from starvation and poor nutrition. Hassan Adamu says opponents of GM food are misguided. He believes GM food has the potential for saving many lives. "If we take

Above: This genetically modified golden rice has a high vitamin A content.

their alarmist warnings [about GM food] to heart, millions of Africans will suffer and possibly die. Agricultural biotechnology...holds great promise for Africa and other areas of the world where circumstances such as poverty and poor growing conditions make farming difficult."

OBJECTIONS TO GM FOODS

Despite the advantages of GM foods, many environmental and consumer groups object to them. They feel that scientists have not done enough research regarding human health hazards,

environmental concerns, or issues related to society and economics.

One objection is that biotechnology is still an inexact science. Many scientists, as well as consumers, argue that we still don't know what effect these genetic changes could have on future generations. Since potential effects can't yet be predicted, they insist we need far more research.

Even though foods produced through biotechnology are said to be as safe as conventional foods, some countries have not approved GM crops. For example, the United Kingdom, France, and other members of the European Union (EU) do not allow farmers to plant most GM crops there. These nations also do not allow buyers to purchase GM foods from another country. Insect-resistant corn is the one exception. In 2007 eight EU countries planted more than 247,000 acres (99,957 hectares) of insect-resistant corn.

Opponents of biotechnology also have environmental concerns. Researchers from Cornell

University in New York reported that *Bt* corn pollen can kill not just pests but also the larvae of monarch butterflies. But other studies have shown different results. A research study published in the journal *Proceedings of the National Academy of Sciences* in 2001 reported that *Bt* poses almost no threat to monarch populations. Indeed, some evidence suggests *Bt* corn could greatly benefit monarch butterfly survival by reducing overall pesticide use.

Some scientists worry, however, that insects will develop resistance to GM crops, just as some populations of mosquitoes developed resistance to the pesticide DDT. Another concern is that crop plants engineered for herbicide tolerance will cross-breed. This could result in the transfer of the herbicide-resistant genes from the crops into the weeds. These "superweeds" would then be herbicide-tolerant as well. Could biotechnology also create a new species of "superbugs" that are resistant to the pesticides engineered into GM crops? Some scientists think so.

Finally, critics of biotechnology question whether genetic engineering could

Above: Flag-waving protesters in Britain gather at a rally against genetically modified food.

> **A genome [all the genetic material in an organism] is like an ecosystem. When you introduce new things, it can have not so much of an impact or [it can have] a catastrophic impact. Scientists have no control over where the genes go, which can cause all sorts of disruption.**
>
> **–MICHAEL HANSON,** CONSUMER POLICY INSTITUTE,
> USA TODAY, JULY 27, 2005

cause the foods we eat every day to become toxic or carcinogenic (cancer-causing). Worse yet, they believe it could easily take a whole human generation before the full extent of any harmful effects might be known. "The vast majority of foods in supermarkets contain genetically modified substances whose effects on our health are unknown," says Martha R. Herbert, a pediatric neurologist (a doctor who studies the nervous system of children). "As a medical doctor, I can assure you that no one in the medical profession would attempt to perform experiments on human subjects without their consent. Such conduct is illegal and unethical. Yet manufacturers of genetically altered foods are exposing us to one of the largest uncontrolled experiments in modern history."

Other experts insist, however, that GM foods are as safe as foods produced using traditional practices. Proponents point out that biotechnology plants and foods are among the most heavily tested. To date, no approved biotechnology food has harmed human health, they say. Some proponents believe GM foods may be even safer than conventional foods.

Weeds, insects show resistance to biotech

From the Pages of
USA TODAY

At least nine weeds have become resistant to the herbicide used with genetically engineered crops and two insect species have developed resistance to plants genetically engineered to produce their own pesticides, a report by the National Research Council said Tuesday.

Genetically engineered crops, which make up about 80% of the soybeans, corn and cotton grown in the USA, save farmers money and keep dangerous herbicides and pesticides out of the nation's waterways. But if farmers, seed companies and government agencies don't develop better ways to manage how they're used, those benefits could be lost, says the council, which carries out studies for the National Academy of Sciences.

The most popular biotech trait is resistance to glyphosate, an herbicide. These crops can tolerate a dousing with Roundup, which kills weeds, thereby reducing the need for tilling the fields. Also popular are crops with a gene from a naturally occurring soil bacteria called *Bacillus thuringiensis* (*Bt*) added so they can produce their own pesticide.

ORGANIC VERSUS GM

Organic farming prohibits the growing of GM foods. A National Organic Program regulation states: "The use of genetically engineered organisms and their products are prohibited in any form or at any stage in organic production, processing or handling." The organic food industry has campaigned against genetically modified crops. The industry believes that GM crops are dangerous for human health. They say that animals that eat genetically modified organisms are developing more diseases.

Organic farmers worry that GM seeds will become widespread. Carried by the wind and birds, they will contaminate neighboring farms and ruin the organic farming industry.

"In general we find that genetically engineered crops have had fewer adverse effects on the environment than non-genetically engineered crops produced conventionally," says LaReesa Wolfenbarger, a professor of biology at the University of Nebraska–Omaha and member of the panel that produced the report.

Problems have arisen, however. Though the genes for herbicide resistance or *Bt* production don't flow from crops to weeds or insects, classic natural evolution is producing resistance: Those that can't survive exposure to glyphosate or *Bt* die, and those that can live to pass on their genes.

The government needs to do a better job of making sure farmers and seed companies develop and follow rules to keep the technology working, says Gregory Jaffe, biotechnology director at the Center for Science in the Public Interest in Washington, D.C. Otherwise it will be "squandered away. We'll be trading short-term gains for a long-term loss."

Groups opposed to genetically engineered crops called the report disappointing. It "fails to appreciate the inherent unsustainability [natural long-term failure] of the pesticide-promoting technologies being offered by the industry," says Andrew Kimbrell, director of the non-profit Center for Food Safety in Washington, D.C.

–Elizabeth Weise

Yet, GM proponents point to studies that show that Bt corn is even safer than organically grown corn. According to the Pesticide Information Office at the University of Florida, "*Bt* corn has been discovered to contain on average 900 percent less cancer-causing mycotoxins than the non-GM corn variety grown by organic and traditional farmers."

FUTURE OF GM FOODS

Advocates of GM foods maintain that this technology holds great promise for the world's food supply. On the other hand, critics say it is too early to conclude that GM foods are safe. Yet, there is some common ground. Both sides agree that further research into the safety and nutritional value of GM food is in everyone's best interest.

CHAPTER SEVEN

The Future of Agriculture

WHEN YOU HEAR THE WORD ORGANIC, THINK STAR-vation," said Earl L. Butz, U.S. secretary of agriculture in the 1970s. In that decade, most people agreed with Earl Butz. They generally had a negative attitude about organic food production. Yet, in the twenty-first century, sales of organic food and beverages have grown significantly. In 1990 sales amounted to $1 billion for the year. By 2009 sales had increased to $24.8 billion each year. In addition, from 2000 through 2008, sales of organic foods increased by 20 percent annually.

Land in the United States that is certified organic has also expanded significantly. In 2008 it reached more than 4.8 million acres (1.9 million hectares). That includes 2.7 million acres (1.1 million hectares) of organic cropland. It also includes 2.1 million acres (850 million hectares) of organic pastureland. How does that compare with 1990? That was the year when Congress passed the Organic Foods Production Act. Back then,

Left: A member of a community-supported agriculture (CSA) program picks up his weekly share of organic produce. Although the local and organic agriculture movements are growing rapidly in the United States, they still are comparatively small.

" **When we buy organic, we're subscribing to a different kind of environment ethic, and we're treating the people who grow our food better.** "

−MARK KASTEL, COFOUNDER, CORNUCOPIA INSTITUTE

USA TODAY · DECEMBER 21, 2010

USA TODAY Snapshots®

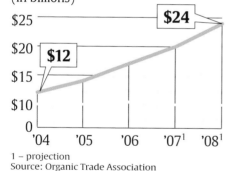

Fast growth

Organic food sales in the U.S. have grown rapidly since 1990 when the market was estimated at $1 billion. (in billions)

1 – projection
Source: Organic Trade Association

By Veronica Salazar, USA TODAY, 2008

3,500 organic farms in California, 1,400 in Wisconsin, and 1,200 in Washington. Those three states have the largest number of organic farms in the United States. But how do the total sales of organic food products compare to the sales of all food products? It is only a small percentage. In 2009, for example, sales of organic food products amounted to $25 billion. That was only 3.7 percent of all food and beverage sales that year. At the same time, certified organic farmland represented only about 0.7 percent of all American cropland. And only 0.5 percent of all pastures were certified organic.

the United States had fewer than 1 million acres (405 million hectares) of organic farmland.

Nearly 13,000 farms throughout the country have been certified organic by the USDA. These include more than

U.S. Organic Cropland

Between 2005 and 2008, the number of acres of certified organic cropland grew slightly. Yet, the number is still a small percent of all cropland in the United States. Below are some crops and the percent of cropland that is certified organic.

Crop	% of all cropland 2005	% of all cropland 2008
Corn	0.16	0.21
Wheat	0.48	0.69
Rice	0.78	1.80
Tomatoes	1.62	2.13
Apples	3.35	4.62

Above: An organic farmer stands among his crops near San Francisco, California, in 2007. California has the largest number of certified organic farms in the United States.

Organic agriculture is still in its infancy. Yet, many agriculturalists believe that is about to change. What exactly is the future for agriculture in the United States? Agriculturalists, economists, and consumers see two possible paths.

INDUSTRIALIZATION

One path is the continuation of the industrialization of agriculture that began at the end of World War II. Industrialization brought about major changes in agriculture.

At the beginning of the century, nearly half the jobs in the United States were on small farms in rural areas. These farms were diversified. They produced a variety of crops, livestock, or both on a small family-owned farm.

By the beginning of the twenty-first century, however, fewer than 2 percent of people in the United States earned their living by working on farms or in agriculture. The large number of small farms had almost disappeared. A small number of large farms had taken their place.

These farms were often specialized. They grew one particular crop or livestock. And they were owned by large corporations, known as agribusinesses.

For example, in 1967 the United States had more than 1 million hog farms. Thirty years later, in 1997, that number had fallen to fewer than 157,000. That's because these agribusinesses had bought out the smaller farms. As a result, the largest 3 percent of these corporate-owned farms produced 60 percent of U.S. hogs.

The much larger farms became possible because of advances in technology. Before the 1950s, crops were harvested by hand. By the 1970s, most crops were harvested by mechanical means. In addition, scientists developed new methods for breeding livestock and growing crops. The result was greater productivity (the rate and quantity of what is produced).

The industrialization of American farms helped lower the cost of food to consumers. Large agribusinesses buy

Above: Because agribusinesses have bought out so many of them, small hog farms like this one have become hard to find in the United States.

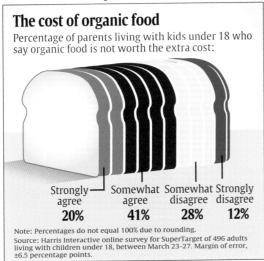

USA TODAY Snapshots®

The cost of organic food

Percentage of parents living with kids under 18 who say organic food is not worth the extra cost:

Strongly agree	Somewhat agree	Somewhat disagree	Strongly disagree
20%	41%	28%	12%

Note: Percentages do not equal 100% due to rounding.
Source: Harris Interactive online survey for SuperTarget of 496 adults living with children under 18, between March 23-27. Margin of error, ±6.5 percentage points.

By Mary Cadden and Alejandro Gonzalez, USA TODAY, 2006

supplies, such as feed for cattle, in great quantities. Because they purchase so much, these large-scale farms can also bargain for lower prices. The agribusinesses were able to pass their cost savings on to the consumer.

Many experts wonder if agribusinesses may move their farm production to foreign countries to save even more money.

Future "Organic" Farmers of America

In 1928 a group of young farmers started a farm education organization. They called it Future Farmers of America (FFA). Their goal was clear. They wanted to help future generations meet the challenges of feeding the world's growing population.

Sixty years later, the name was changed to the National FFA Organization. Members feel that this name is better for one main reason. It reflects the diversity of the agricultural industry. The organization is inspiring a new "crop" of young agriculturalists. They are young American farmers who will have the training and expertise to lead the next American farming revolution.

Yet, many people are concerned. They fear that young people are not getting the needed skills and training in organic agriculture. They feel that future farmers need to have better skills and knowledge in soil ecology. They also believe that future farmers need to know more about organic greenhouse production (growing organic crops year-round in greenhouses). Finally, farmers need to understand composting practices (use of decaying organic matter for fertilizer).

Economist Steven Blank is the author of *The End of Agriculture in the American Portfolio*. He says that like U.S. industrial production, farming may also be outsourced. This is because materials and labor are far cheaper in other countries. Blank writes that "the production of food and other agricultural products will disappear from the United States because it will become unprofitable to tie up resources in farming and ranching."

SUSTAINABLE AGRICULTURE

But there is another path. That path has its roots in

Ryan Zinn is national campaign coordinator for the Organic Consumers Association. He is particularly concerned about the lack of organic agriculture education. "Quite frankly, there just are not enough organic farmers out there that have the technical skills to meet the demand," Zinn says.

Yet, there are promising signs for the future. In 2000 no college or university in North America offered a course in organic agriculture. That year, however, 350 students at an agricultural college in Canada sent a petition to the administration. They wanted an organic agriculture course at the college. Two years later, the first organic course was offered at the school. Two years after that, in 2004, the agricultural college became the first school in North America to establish an organic agriculture major.

A number of universities and colleges in the United States now offer courses in organic agriculture. In 2006 Washington State University became the first university in the United States to establish an organic agriculture major. The organic food industry is growing. As it does, future graduates in organic agriculture will help fulfill the goals set so many years ago by the founders of FFA.

sustainable agriculture. This is a method of farming that does not damage, destroy, or deplete the soil or environment. John Ikerd, a retired professor of agricultural economics at the University of Missouri–Columbia, has written extensively about sustainable agriculture. As he sees it, the new American farm is about three specific things. It's about "environmental integrity, about economic viability, and about social responsibility." But ultimately, Ikerd says, the new American farm is about people.

On tiny plots, a new generation of farmers emerges

<u>From the Pages of</u>
<u>USA TODAY</u>

Joseph Gabiou walks the fields of Wobbly Cart Farming Collective with a practiced eye. He kicks dirt into place to keep the wind from blowing the protective covering off a row of organic broccoli. The seedlings are vulnerable to the flea beetles that came in the spring, just as longtime farmers in this valley told him they would.

To a new farmer, that's crucial information. The farm, started five years ago, is young. But so is the 33-year-old Gabiou at a time when the average age of the American farmer is 57, according to the Department of Agriculture. The 2007 agriculture census found that more than one-quarter of all farmers are 65 or older.

Wobbly Cart is also tiny, just 6 acres [2.5 hectares]. Nationwide, the average farm is 449 acres [182 hectares].

But Gabiou and business partner Asha McElfresh, 32, differ from typical farmers in another way. Wobbly Cart, say agriculture specialists, is part of a movement in which young people—most of whom come from cities and suburbs—are taking up what may be the world's oldest profession: organic farming.

"I'm seeing an enthusiastic group of young people all across the country who want to get into farming," says Fred Kirschenmann, a longtime farmer and fellow at the Leopold Center for Sustainable Agriculture at Iowa State University in Ames.

The wave of young farmers on tiny farms is too new and too small to have turned up significantly in USDA statistics, but people in the farming world acknowledge there's something afoot.

For these new farmers, going back to the land isn't a rejection of conventional society, but an embrace of growing crops and raising animals for market as an honorable, important career choice—one that's been waning since 1935, when the U.S. farms peaked at 6.8 million.

It's about creating something real—the food people eat—and at the same time healing the Earth, says Severine von Tscharner Fleming, 27, a farmer in Nevis, N.Y. "The America that I want to live in will support people who are willing to work [very hard], who want to do good things for their community. We're patriots of place. Here I am, I'm planting my trees."

Three factors have made these small, organic farms possible: a rising consumer demand for organic and local produce, a huge increase in farmers markets nationwide, and the growing popularity of community-supported agriculture (CSA) programs.

CSAs are programs that allow consumers to buy a share of a farm's output for one year. The farmer gets an assured income stream [money they can count on], and the consumer gets a box of produce delivered once a week during the growing season. Shares generally range from $25 to $50 a week.

The economics [of small organic farms] can be brutal. "Most first-generation young farmers work another job for a decade or more, and/or have a spouse who works full time," says [Cornell agriculture professor Ian Merwin].

Jennifer Belknap, 36, and her husband, Jim McGinn, 43, are old-timers. Their Rochester, Wash., farm, Rising River, dates to 1994. Belknap estimates they net $30,000 a year. They live off the land and keep other expenses to a minimum.

It's like "being a ninja," says Fleming, in Nevis, N.Y. You have to be fluid, flexible, an activist and an entrepreneur, she says. "We're working against the odds. The educational system, the economic system, the subsidies [government money to help farmers], the tax structure for landowners," none of them are focused on helping tiny organic farmers, she says.

Because very few [of these young farmers] grew up on farms, most get the skills they need by interning, apprenticing or working on other farms.

Belknap, originally from Norman, Okla., says Rising River Farm gets its share of "idealistic barefooted gardeners" who don't get that farming is hard work. But they keep coming, and she's proud to say several new farmers began their career there.

It's wonderful to do what you love, she says, but no one should imagine it's romantic and glamorous. "We used to pull bags for our vegetables from the recycling. One of the jobs for the interns was sniffing the bags" to see if they were too smelly to use.

–Elizabeth Weise

Above: A farmer tosses a cantaloupe to a buyer at a New York City farmers market. This market only includes vendors with certified organic produce, grains, and meats. The number of farmers who sell directly to consumers is rising.

These American farms, Ikerd also says, go by many different names. They include organic, natural, ecological, or just plain family farms. But they all have the same core principles: "First, these farmers...work with nature rather than try to control or conquer nature.... Second, these new farmers build relationships. They tend to have more direct contact with their customers than do conventional farmers. They produce the things that their customers value most, rather than try to convince their customers to buy whatever they produce.... Finally, for these new farmers...their 'quality of life' objectives are at least as important as the economic objectives in carrying out their farming operations."

Doug Gurian-Sherman, senior scientist at the Union of Concerned Scientists, he agrees with Ikerd. He also believes that

> **When we said organic, we meant local. We meant healthful. We meant being true to the ecologies of regions. We meant mutually respectful growers and eaters. We meant social justice and equality.**
>
> **–JOAN DYE GUSSOW,** RETIRED PROFESSOR OF NUTRITION AT COLUMBIA UNIVERSITY IN NEW YORK
>
> USA TODAY · OCTOBER 28, 2002

future farmers have only one way to produce enough food efficiently and economically for the world. It is by working with nature—not through continued industrialization of agriculture. "Promising methods and technologies like organic are in the vanguard [cutting edge] of that effort," Gurian-Sherman says.

Will the future of American agriculture follow the principles and beliefs of organic agriculture? Andrew Kimbrell, director of the Center for Food Safety, sums up the debate with these words: "We find ourselves in the midst of a historic battle between two very different visions of the future of food in the twenty-first century. The decades-long domination of the industrial model of food production is now being challenged by a strong grassroots movement in favor of organic, ecological, and humane food." Which one will win out? Which one should win out? Study and weigh the facts, and then you decide.

NORFOLK PUBLIC LIBRARY
NORFOLK, NEBRASKA

TIMELINE

CIRCA 10,000 B.C.   Early development of agriculture begins.

1840   German chemist Justus von Liebig (1803–1873), known as the father of the fertilizer industry, identifies three major chemicals (nitrogen [N], phosphorus [P], and potassium [K]) that all plants need to grow.

1939   Lady Evelyn (Eve) Balfour (1899–1990) of Britain launches the Haughley Experiment, a thirty-year-long scientific comparison of organic farming versus conventional farming.

1940   British agriculturalist Lord Northbourne (1896–1982) uses the term *organic farming* in his book *Look to the Land*. The term is based on his concept of the farm as an organism.

1940s   Widespread use of chemical fertilizers begins in the United States and around the world.

1942   J. I. Rodale starts the organic movement with the publication of his magazine *Organic Farming and Gardening*.

1943   Organic farming pioneer Sir Albert Howard (1873–1947), father of modern composting, publishes *An Agricultural Testament*, the classic text on soil fertility. The book lays the foundation for the organic agriculture movement.

1962   Rachel Carson (1907–1964) publishes *Silent Spring*, said to have inspired the start of the environmental movement. Her book is also a turning point for interest in modern organic farming.

1969   President Richard Nixon appoints a committee to consider whether there should be a separate environmental agency.

1970   The U.S. Environmental Protection Agency (EPA), charged with protecting human health and the environment, begins operations.

1970   A group of California farmers form the first organization to certify organic farms in North America.

1971   Earl L. Butz (1909–2008) becomes secretary of agriculture under President Nixon: Butz becomes a strong advocate for large agribusinesses.

1972   The U.S. Congress bans the use of the pesticide DDT in the United States.

The U.S. Congress passes the Clean Water Act, a set of laws designed to regulate water pollution in the United States.

1979   California passes the first law establishing legal standards for organic production.

1980   The USDA publishes a ninety-four-page document, *Report and Recommendations on Organic Farming.* Garth Youngberg is appointed the USDA's first organic farming coordinator.

Wes Jackson (1936–) is credited with the first use of the term *sustainable agriculture* in his book *New Roots for Agriculture.*

1990   The U.S. Congress passes the Organic Foods Production Act, which authorizes the USDA to develop and implement standards for the production and processing of organic food.

1994   The world's first GM crop, the Flav Savr tomato, is approved by the Food and Drug Administration (FDA) for human consumption.

2002   The USDA implements National Organic Program (NOP) standards, twelve years after Congress passed the Organic Foods Production Act of 1990.

The world's first organic agriculture course is offered at a university in North America (University of Guelph, Ontario, Canada).

2009 President Barack Obama issues a new executive order that prevents processors from slaughtering downed cattle (cattle that are not able to stand, either through illness or disease) for human food.

First Lady Michelle Obama plants an organic vegetable garden on the White House lawn.

2010 Maria Rodale, granddaughter of J. I. Rodale and CEO and chairman of Rodale Inc., publishes *Organic Manifesto: How Organic Farming Can Heal Our Planet, Feed the World, and Keep Us Safe.*

The organic food industry grows by 8 percent in 2010, dramatically outpacing the food industry as a whole, which grew at less than 1 percent in 2010.

2011 U.S. secretary of agriculture Tom Vilsack declares organic farming an important part of the strategy to rebuild rural America.

GLOSSARY

agribusiness: a large-scale farming operation that includes production, processing, and distribution of agricultural products

antibiotic: a substance that destroys or inhibits the growth of harmful organisms, especially bacteria. Farmers often give antibiotics to livestock to prevent illnesses among the animals and to promote growth.

antibiotic resistance: the condition in which bacteria or other harmful organisms are not killed by a specific antibiotic because the organism has developed resistance to (defense against) that particular antibiotic

beneficial species: an organism that helps a crop by eating or otherwise controlling pests or weeds that attack or crowd out the crop

biotechnology: using scientific methods to alter living things to produce useful and commercial products such as GM foods or drugs for medical use

compost: decayed organic matter. Compost is used as a soil conditioner and as a fertilizer.

Concentrated Animal Feeding Operation (CAFO): facilities where animals raised for food are kept in confined spaces

DDT (dichlorodiphenyltrichloroethane): a synthetic pesticide. Because of its extreme toxicity to humans and to the environment, DDT was banned in the United States in 1972.

E. coli (Escherichia coli): a species of disease-causing bacteria that lives in the intestines of people and other vertebrates

factory farm: a large-scale facility where large numbers of animals are raised for food. The animals are confined and treated with hormones and antibiotics to maximize growth and prevent disease.

feedlot: a type of animal-feeding operation, such as a CAFO

fertilizer: a substance that farmers add to agricultural lands to encourage plant growth and to raise crop production

genetically modified organism (GMO): a plant, an animal, or a microorganism that is transformed by altering its genetic makeup; also called a genetically engineered organism (GEO)

humus: a dark, soil-like material that comes from composting organic matter. Humus contains plant nutrients and is often spread on cropland to improve the fertility of the soil.

lagoon: a shallow artificial pond for holding liquefied animal waste

organic: a plant, an animal, or a food product that is grown or manufactured without pesticides, herbicides, antibiotics, or hormones

organophosphates: a group of chemicals originally developed for chemical warfare. The chemicals are also used in insecticides and herbicides.

pesticide: a chemical used to prevent, destroy, or repel pests

pollutant: any substance that causes harm to air, water, or soil

ruminant: a mammal whose stomach has four parts to digest the plant-based food it eats. Cattle, sheep, goats, deer, and elk are ruminants.

sustainable agriculture: farming methods that do not damage, destroy, or deplete the soil or the environment

SOURCE NOTES

6 Bonnie McCarvel and Janet Braum, "MACA Letter to White House about Organic Garden," CropLife.com, March 31, 2009, http://www.croplife.com/news/?storyid=1657 (December 27, 2010).

7 Rob Lyons, "The Truth about Organic Food," *Spiked*, January 9, 2007, http://www.spiked-online.com/index.php?/site/boxarticle/2691/ (December 27, 2010).

7 Nina Fedoroff, "A Little Common Sense, Please," FBAE, June 18, 2009, http://fbae.org/2009/FBAE/website/news_09_07_a-little-common-sense-please.html (December 27, 2010).

9–10 Maria Rodale, *Organic Manifesto: How Organic Farming Can Heal Our Planet, Feed the World, and Keep Us Safe* (New York: Rodale, 2010), 4.

10 Frances Moore Lappé and Anna Lappé, "The Food Crisis and the Fear of Scarcity," FAIR, November–December 2008, http://www.fair.org/index.php?page=3704 (December 27, 2010).

15 Albert Howard, *An Agricultural Testament* (New York: Oxford University Press, 1943), 37.

15–16 Ibid.

16 Ibid.

17 Lady Eve Balfour, "Towards a Sustainable Agriculture—The Living Soil Part 2," *Organic NZ*, May–June 2001, http://www.organicnz.org/organic-nz-magazine/1132/towards-a-sustainable-agriculture-the-living-soil-part-2/ (December 28, 2010).

19 Wade Green, "Guru of the Organic Food Cult," *New York Times Magazine*, June 6, 1971, http://select.nytimes.com/gst/abstract.html?res=F70A12FE3D5E127A93C4A9178DD85F458785F9&scp=1&sq=Guru+of+the+organic+food+cult&st=p (December 28, 2010).

22 Joseph J. Heckman, "A History of Organic Farming: Transitions from Sir Albert Howard's War in the Soil to USDA National Organic Program," *Renewable Agriculture and Food Systems* 21 (2006):143–150, available online at http://aesop.rutgers.edu/~plantbiopath/faculty/heckman/heckman.html (December 28, 2010).

23 Roger Blobaum, "USDA Had an Organic Farming Coordinator in 1980; Call for Reinstatement Now Made 30 Years Later," *Organic Broadcaster*, March–April 2010, http://www.mosesorganic.org/attachments/broadcaster/roger18.2usdafarmcoordinator.html (December 28, 2010).

25 WhoRunsGov.com, "Profile: Tom Vilsack," The Washington Post, 2010, http://www.whorunsgov.com/Profiles/Tom_Vilsack (December 28, 2010).

27 Aurora Organic Dairy, 2010, http://www.auroraorganic.com (June 4, 2010).

27 Ibid.

28–29 Organic Guide, "Mark Retzloff from Aurora Organic Dairy," n.d., http://www.organicguide.com/organic/people/mark-retzloff-from-aurora-organic-dairy (December 27, 2010).

29 Anita Manning, "USDA Gives Bite to Organic Label," USA Today, October 15, 2002.

35 Organic Consumers Association, "National Organic Standards on Outdoor Access/Pasture Requirements for Organic Animals/Livestock," OCA, October 21, 2005, http://www.organicconsumers.org/sos/livestock102405.cfm (December 27, 2010).

36 Elizabeth Aguilera, "Aurora Organic Dairy under Scrutiny," denverpost.com, January 27, 2008, http://www.denverpost.com/business/ci_8083332 (December 27, 2010).

37 Elizabeth Weise, "'Organic' Milk Needs a Pasture; USDA Ruling on Grazing Is Latest Round in Debate," USA Today, March 9, 2005.

37 Ibid.

37 Ibid.

37 Organic Guide, "Mark Retzloff."]

39 "James's ADHD Story," AdhdNews.com, n.d., http://www.adhdnews.com/adhd-testimonials-james.htm (December 28, 2010).

41 Environmental Working Group, "Why Should You Care about Pesticides?" WG, 2010, http://www.foodnews.org/EWG-shoppers-guide-download-final.pdf (December 28, 2010).

41 Hembree Brandon, "Pesticides and ADHD," Western Farm Press, June 5, 2010, http://westernfarmpress.com/news/pesticides-adhd-0615 (December 28, 2010).

41 Ibid.

43 "Organic Foods Really Do Have Less Pesticides: New Study from Consumers Union," press release, Mindfully.org, May 8, 2002, http://www.mindfully.org/Food/Organic-Less-Pesticides8may02.htm#1 (December 28, 2010).

44 Alex Avery, The Truth about Organic Foods (Chesterfield, MO: Henderson Communications, 2006), as quoted in Rob Lyons, "The Truth about Organic Food," Spiked, January 9, 2007, http://www.spiked-online.com/index.php?/site/article/2691/ (April 15, 2011).

45 Leo Horrigan, Robert S. Lawrence, and Polly Walker, "How Sustainable Agriculture Can Address the Environmental and Human Health Harms of Industrial Agriculture," *Environmental Health Perspectives*, May 2002, http://ehp03.niehs.nih.gov/article/fetchArticle.action?articleURI=info:doi/10.1289/ehp.02110445 (December 28, 2010).

45 Suzanne H. Reuben, President's Cancer Panel, *Reducing Environmental Cancer Risk: What We Can Do Now*, April 2010, http://deainfo.nci.nih.gov/advisory/pcp/annualReports/pcp08-09rpt/PCP_Report_08-09_508.pdf (October 9, 2010).

45 Ibid.

48 Charles Benbrook, "New Evidence Confirms the Nutritional Superiority of Plant-Based Organic Foods," Organic Center, March 2008, http://www.organic-center.org/science.nutri.php?action=view&report_id=126 (December 28, 2010).

48 Joseph Rosen, "Organic Center Should Admit: Organic Not More Nutritious," American Council on Science and Health, August 8, 2008, http://www.acsh.org/factsfears/newsID.1179/news_detail.asp (December 28, 2010).

49 Rebecca Ruiz, "Organic Food: Behind the Hype," Forbes.com, August 8, 2009, http://www.forbes.com/2009/08/20/organic-foods-facts-lifestyle-health-organic-products.html (December 28, 2010).

49 Mary V. Gold, "Does Organically-Grown Food Contain More or Better Nutrients—Vitamins, Minerals, and Phytonutrients—Than Conventionally Grown Food?" USDA, National Agricultural Library, October 2008, http://www.nal.usda.gov/afsic/pubs/faq/BuyOrganicFoodsB.shtml (December 28, 2010).

52 J. Gordon Edwards, "The Lies of Rachel Carson," *21st Century Science & Technology Magazine*, Summer 1992, http://www.21stcenturysciencetech.com/articles/summ02/Carson.html (December 27, 2010).

52 Lisa Budwig, "Breaking Nature's Silence: Pennsylvania's Rachel Carson," *Pennsylvania Heritage*, Fall 1992, available online at http://www.rachelcarsonhomestead.org/Education/FeaturedStoriesandReports/BreakingNaturesSilence/tabid/86/Default.aspx (December 27, 2010).

52 Dorothy McLaughlin, "*Silent Spring* Revisited," *Fooling with Nature, Frontline* Online, 2010, http://www.pbs.org/wgbh/pages/frontline/shows/nature/disrupt/sspring.html (December 27, 2010).

53 Budwig, "Breaking."

53 Michael Roston, "Republican Environmental Critic Blocks Honors for Rachel Carson, Author of *Silent Spring*," the *Raw Story*, May 22, 2007, http://www.rawstory.com/news/2007/Senator_blocks_honors_for_Rachel_Carson_0522.html (December 27, 2010).

56 Angela Logomasini, "Rachel Carson's Deadly Legacy," Op Ed, the *Washington Times*, May 31, 2007, available online at http://cei.org/gencon/019,05945.cfm (December 27, 2010).

56 Ronald Bailey, "*Silent Spring* at 40," *Reason*, June 12, 2002, http://reason.com/archives/2002/06/12/silent-spring-at-40 (September 24, 2010).

60 U.S. Geological Survey, *The Quality of Our Nation's Waters: Pesticides in the Nation's Streams and Ground Water, 1992–2001* (Reston, VA: USGS, 2007), http://pubs.usgs.gov/circ/2005/1291/pdf/circ1291_chapter1.pdf (December 27, 2010).

61 George Kuepper and Lance Gegner, "Organic Crop Production Overview," National Sustainable Agriculture Information Service, August 2004, http://attra.ncat.org/attra-pub/PDF/organiccrop.pdf#xml=http://search.ncat.org/texis/search/pdfhi.txt?query=amount+of+grain+produced&pr=ATTRA2010&prox=page&rorder=500&rprox=500&rdfreq=500&rwfreq=500&rlead=500&rdepth=0&sufs=0&order=r&cq=&id=4d74bb5742 (March 4, 2011).

61 U.S. Environmental Protection Agency, "Are Pesticides Safe?" n.d., http://pesticides.supportportal.com/ics/support/default.asp?deptID=23008 (December 27, 2010).

63 John Quiggin and Tim Lambert, "Rehabilitating Carson," *Prospect*, May 24, 2008, http://www.prospectmagazine.co.uk/2008/05/rehabilitatingcarson (December 29, 2010).

66 Sustainable Dictionary, "Feedlots," Sustainable Table, n.d., http://www.sustainabletable.org/intro/dictionary/ (December 30, 2010).

67 Meat Industry Insights News Service, "USDA Inspector Claims Cattle, Pigs Brutalized," *Meat Industry Insights*, April 1, 1998, http://www.spcnetwork.com/mii/1998/980413.htm (December 30, 2010).

67 Humane Farming Association, "Factory Farming: The True Costs," HFA, n.d., http://www.all-creatures.org/articles/ar-factoryfarming.html (December 30, 2010).

69 Region 7 Concentrated Animal Feeding Operations, "How Do CAFOs Impact the Environment?" U.S. Environmental Protection Agency, n.d., http://www.epa.gov/region7/water/cafo/cafo_impact_environment (December 30, 2010).

71 National Cattlemen's Beef Association, "Producer Code of Cattle Care," Beef USA, 2010, http://www.beefusa.org/NEWSProducerCodeofCattleCare35181.aspx (December 30, 2010).

75 Administrator, "Myths & Facts about Animal Agriculture," Growing IN Agriculture, January 18, 2007, http://www.growinginagriculture. com/index.php?option=com_content&task=view&id=68&Itemid=9 (December 30, 2010).

75 *Antibiotic Resistance: Federal Agencies Need to Better Focus Efforts to Address Risk to Humans from Antibiotic Use in Animals,* (Washington, DC: U.S. Government Accountability Office), http://gao.gov/products/GAO-04-490 (December 30, 2010).

75 "Antibiotic Use in Cattle Production," fact sheet, Explore Beef, 2010, http://explorebeef.org/CMDocs/ExploreBeef/FactSheet_AntibioticUseInCattleProduction.pdf (December 30, 2010).

77 Cattlemen's Beef Board and National Cattlemen's Beef Association, "Common Potential Concerns About Today's Beef Production," Explore Beef, 2009, http://explorebeef.org/raisingbeef.aspx (December 27, 2009).

77 Cattlemen's Beef Board and National Cattlemen's Beef Association, "Nick Hunt," Explore Beef, 2009, http://www.explorebeef.org/huntfamily.aspx (December 30, 2009).

81 Ronnie Cummins, "Generation Monsanto," *Huffington Post,* June 21, 2010, http://www.huffingtonpost.com/ronnie-cummins/generation-monsanto-gm_b_619561.html (December 29, 2010).

82 Krista Weider, "As More Genetically Modified Foods Reach the Marketplace, What Does the Future Hold?" Pakissan, n.d., http://www.pakissan.com/english/advisory/biotechnology/as.more.genetically.modified.shtml (December 29, 2010).

84 Elizabeth Weise, "Technology Creates a Standoff on Farms," *USA Today,* March 17, 2010.

84 Hassan Adamu, "We'll Feed Our People as We See Fit," *Washington Post,* September 11, 2000, http://www.highbeam.com/doc/1P2-545421.html (December 29, 2010).

87 Martha Herbert, "Genetically Altered Foods: We Are Being Exposed to One of the Largest Uncontrolled Experiments in History," *Chicago Tribune,* September 3, 2000, http://www.mindfully.org/GE/Uncontrolled-Experiment3sep00.htm (December 29, 2010).

88 National Organic Program, USDA.org, n.d., http://www.ams.usda.gov/AMSv1.0/nop (December 30, 2010).

89 University of Florida, "Organic vs. GM," Pesticide Information Office, May 9, 2007, http://www.pested.ifas.ufl.edu/newsletters/may2007/organic.htm (December 30, 2010).

91 Jim Slama, "Food of the Future," Organic Consumers Association, March 28, 2002, http://www.organicconsumers.org/Organic/future042202.cfm (December 31, 2010).

96 Steven C. Blank, *The End of Agriculture in the American Portfolio.* Westport, CT: Quorum Books, 1998, 1.

97 Nancy Pfoutz, "Universities Launching Organic Farming Programs," The Organic & Non-GMO Report, November 2006, http://www.non-gmoreport. com/articles/nov06/organic_farming.php (December 31, 2010).

97 John Ikerd, "Painting a New Picture: The New American Farm," paper, presented at the Annual Meeting of Community Farm Alliance, Lexington, KY, January 12, 2002, http://web.missouri.edu/~ikerdj/papers/NewPicture.html (December 31, 2010).

100 John Ikerd, "Why Farming Is Important in America," a paper presented at the Fourth Annual Rural Development conference, February 5–7, 2002, http://web .missouri.edu/ikerdj/papers/WhyFarming.html (December 31, 2010).

101 Doug Gurian-Sherman, "Organic Agriculture Is the Future," Organic Consumers Association, June 12, 2009, http://www.organicconsumers.org/ articles/article_18699.cfm (December 31, 2010).

101 Andrew Kimbrell ed. *Fatal Harvest: The Tragedy of Industrial Agriculture* (Sausalito, CA: Foundation for Deep Ecology, 2002), front flap.

SELECTED BIBLIOGRAPHY

Avery, Alex. *The Truth about Organic Foods.* Chesterfield, MO: Henderson Communications, 2006.

Blank, Steven C. *The End of Agriculture in the American Portfolio.* Westport, CT: Quorum Books, 1998.

Heckman, Joseph J. "A History of Organic Farming: Transitions from Sir Albert Howard's War in the Soil to USDA National Organic Program." *Renewable Agriculture and Food Systems 21*, (2006):143–150. Available online at http://aesop.rutgers.edu/~plantbiopath/faculty/heckman/heckman.html.

Horrigan, Leo, Robert S. Lawrence, and Polly Walker. "How Sustainable Agriculture Can Address the Environmental and Human Health Harms of Industrial Agriculture." *Environmental Health Perspectives*, May 2002. http://ehp03.niehs.nih.gov/article/fetchArticle.action?articleURI=info:doi/10.1289/ehp.02110445 (December 28, 2010).

Howard, Albert. *An Agricultural Testament.* New York: Oxford University Press, 1943.

———. *The Soil and Health: A Study of Organic Agriculture.* Lexington, KY: University Press of Kentucky, 2007.

Kimbrell, Andrew, ed. *Fatal Harvest: The Tragedy of Industrial Agriculture.* Sausalito, CA: Foundation for Deep Ecology, 2002.

Kristiansen, Paul, Acram Taji, and John Reganold, ed. *Organic Agriculture: A Global Perspective.* Ithaca, NY: Comstock Publishing Associates, 2006.

Pew Commission on Industrial Farm Animal Production. "Putting Meat on the Table: Industrial Farm Animal Production in America." Washington, DC: Pew Charitable Trusts and Johns Hopkins Bloomberg School of Public Health, 2008. http://www.pewtrusts.org/uploadedFiles/wwwpewtrustsorg/Reports/Industrial_Agriculture/PCIFAP_FINAL.pdf (May 12, 2011).

Rodale, Maria. *Organic Manifesto: How Organic Farming Can Heal Our Planet, Feed the World, and Keep Us Safe.* New York: Rodale, 2010.

U.S. Geological Survey. *The Quality of Our Nation's Waters: Pesticides in the Nation's Streams and Ground Water, 1992–2001.* Reston, VA: USGS, 2007.

U.S. Government Accountability Office. *Antibiotic Resistance: Federal Agencies Need to Better Focus Efforts to Address Risk to Humans from Antibiotic Use in Animals.* Washington, DC: U.S. Government Accountability Office, 2004. http://gao.gov/products/GAO-04-490 (December 30, 2010).

ORGANIZATIONS TO CONTACT

Agricultural Retailers Association (ARA)

1156 15th Ave. NW, Suite 302
Washington, DC 20005
http://www.aradc.org
The mission of ARA is to support its members in their quest to maintain a profitable business environment, adapt to a changing world, and preserve their freedom to operate.

American Council on Science and Health (ACSH)

1995 Broadway
New York, NY 10023
212-362-7044
http://www.acsh.org
ACSH is a nonprofit consumer education consortium concerned with issues related to food, nutrition, chemicals, pharmaceuticals, the environment, and health.

BIO (Biotechnology Industry Organization)

1201 Maryland Ave. SW
Suite 900
Washington, DC 20024
http://www.bio.org
BIO is the world's largest biotechnology organization, providing advocacy, business development, and communications services for more than twelve hundred members worldwide.

Center for Food Safety (CFS)

660 Pennsylvania Ave. SE, Suite 302
Washington, DC 20003
202-547-9359
http://www.truefoodnow.org
CFS's mission is to work to protect human health and the environment by curbing the proliferation of harmful food production technologies and by promoting organic and other forms of sustainable agriculture.

The Cornucopia Institute

PO Box 126
Cornucopia, WI 54827
608-625-2042
http://www.cornucopia.org
The Cornucopia Institute's goal is to empower farmers—partnered with consumers—in support of ecologically produced local, organic, and authentic food.

CropLife Foundation

1156 15th St. NW
Washington, DC 20005
202-296-1585
http://www.croplifeamerica.org/croplife-network/foundation
The CropLife Foundation is a nonprofit research and education organization created to promote and advance sustainable agriculture and the environmentally sound use of crop protection products and bioengineered agriculture.

Environmental Protection Agency (EPA)

1200 Pennsylvania Ave. NW
Washington, DC 20460
202-272-0167
http://www.epa.gov
The mission of the EPA is to protect human health and the environment.

Environmental Working Group (EWG)

1436 U Street NW
Suite 100
Washington, DC 20009
202-667-6982
http://www.ewg.org
The Environmental Working Group is a nonprofit advocacy organization founded in 1993 to create awareness of the potential health hazards from toxic contaminants.

Growing IN Agriculture (GINA)

5730 W. 74th St.
Indianapolis, IN 46278
317-347-3620
http://www.growinginagriculture.com
GINA is an education and awareness program with the goal of
increasing soybean meal demand by developing Indiana's livestock
industry in a manner that is environmentally safe, socially responsible,
and economically viable for livestock farmers.

Mid America CropLife Association (MACA)

11327 Gravois Rd.
Suite 201
St. Louis, MO 63126
800-625-2767
http://www.maca.org
MACA's mission is to research public issues relating to crop production
and to work together to improve the crop life cycle via health, safety,
and public education.

National Cattlemen's Beef Association

1301 Pennsylvania Ave. NW
Suite 300
Washington, DC 20004
202-347-0228
http://www.beefusa.org
NCBA is the voice of the cattle industry, the association offers beef
and cattle news, up-to-date beef and cattle research, and food safety
information.

National Center for Food and Agricultural Policy

1616 P St. NW
Washington, DC 20036
202-328-5183
http://www.ncfap.org
The National Center for Food and Agricultural Policy fosters and
conducts objective, nonadvocacy research, analysis, and education
to inform public policy on food, agriculture, natural resources,
environment quality, and rural economics.

National Organic Coalition

845-744-2304

http://www.nationalorganiccoalition.org

This is a nongovernmental alliance of organizations working to provide a Washington voice for farmers, ranchers, environmentalists, consumers, and progressive industry members involved in organic agriculture.

The Organic Center

PO Box 20513

Boulder, CO 80308

303-499-1840

http://www.organic-center.org

The Organic Center's mission is to generate and advance credible science on the health and environmental benefits of organic food and farming and to communicate those benefits to the public.

Organic Consumers Association (OCA)

6771 South Silver Hill Dr.

Finland, MN 55603

218-226-4164

http://organicconsumers.org

OCA is a grassroots, nonprofit, public interest organization campaigning for health, justice, and sustainability.

Organic Trade Association (OTA)

60 Wells St.

Greenfield, MA 01301

413-376-1219

http://www.ota.com

OTA's mission is to promote and protect organic trade to benefit the environment, farmers, the public, and the economy.

U.S. Department of Agriculture (USDA)

1400 Independence Ave. SW

Washington, DC 20250

202-720-2791

http://www.usda.gov

The USDA's mission is to develop and execute federal policy on farming, agriculture, and food.

U.S. Food and Drug Administration (FDA)
10903 New Hampshire Ave.
Silver Spring, MD 20993
888-463-6332
http://www.fda.gov/
FDA is responsible for protecting the public health by assuring the safety, efficacy, and security of human and veterinary drugs, biological products, medical devices, the U.S. food supply, cosmetics, and products that emit radiation.

U.S. Government Accountability Office (GAO)
441 G St. NW
Washington, DC 20548
202-512-3000
http://gao.gov
GAO's mission is to support the U.S. Congress in meeting its constitutional responsibilities by providing Congress with timely information that is objective, fact-based, nonpartisan, and nonideological. This includes providing information about agricultural practices in the United States.

FURTHER INFORMATION

BOOKS

Fridell, Ron. *Genetic Engineering.* Minneapolis: Lerner Publications Company, 2006.
> This book takes a look at the basics of how genes work and at the ways in which science can manipulate genes to create a range of new plants, animals, drugs, and other genetically engineered products.

Ikerd, John E. *Crisis and Opportunity: Sustainability in American Agriculture (Our Sustainable Future).* Lincoln, NE: Bison Books, 2008.
> The author outlines the consequences of agricultural industrialization and then details how we can ensure a sustainable agricultural system in the future.

Imhoff, Daniel, ed. *The CAFO Reader: The Tragedy of Industrial Animal Factories.* Sausalito, CA: Foundation for Deep Ecology, 2010.
> The authors in this anthology of essays about Concentrated Animal Feeding Operations (CAFOs) examine the impact and conditions of factory farms in the United States.

Pollin, Michael. *The Omnivore's Dilemma: A Natural History of Four Meals.* New York: Penguin Press, 2006.
> Pollin examines the social, ethical, and environmental impact of industrial and organic agriculture as he follows the food chains that feed humans from the source to the table.

Ronald, Pamela C., and R. W. Adamchak. *Tomorrow's Table: Organic Farming, Genetics, and the Future of Food.* New York: Oxford University Press, 2008.
> The authors look at genetically engineered (GE) food and how it may affect the food supply of the future.

Seiple, Samantha, and Todd Seiple. *Mutants, Clones, and Killer Corn: Unlocking the Secrets of Biotechnology.* Minneapolis: Twenty-First Century Books, 2005.
> This book follows the field of biotechnology from its origins in selective livestock breeding to future uses, such as growing human organs for transplants and re-creating dinosaurs.

Weber, Karl, ed. *Food, Inc: How Industrial Food Is Making Us Sicker, Fatter, and Poorer and What You Can Do about It*. New York: Public Affairs, 2009.
This book includes thirteen essays by experts in food, nutrition, and the environment. The topics range from the industrialization of our food supply to how organic food is going mainstream to sorting out food facts from fiction.

Woods, Michael, and Mary B. Woods. *Ancient Agricultural Technology: From Sickles to Plows*. Minneapolis: Twenty-First Century Books, 2011.
This book gives readers an overview of the development of farming techniques in ancient cultures around the world and shows how some ancient technologies are still in use in the twenty-first century.

BROCHURES

Kuepper, George, and Lance Gegner. "Organic Crop Production Overview." ATTRA–National Sustainable Agriculture Information Service. 2004. http://attra.ncat.org/attra-pub/organiccrop.html
This brochure provides an overview of the key concepts and practices of certified organic crop production, including the myths and issues that have become associated with organic agriculture.

"Organic Food Standards and Labels: The Facts." USDA Consumer Brochure. http://www.ams.usda.gov/nop/Consumers/brochure.html (April 2002).
This brochure explains all the rules that a farmer must follow to have food labeled organic.

OTA. "Quick Overview: Organic Agriculture and Production." Organic Trade Association. http://www.ota.com/definition/quickoverview.html (2007).
This brochure provides a concise overview of the U.S. National Organic Standards.

WEBSITES

Beefnutrition.org

http://www.beefnutrition.org

This site includes resources, nutrition tools, and learning opportunities about beef, as well as free promotional materials. It also includes information about MyPyramid (http://www.mypyramid.gov/), the USDA's interactive eating plan, as well as classroom activity sheets for kids and Spanish materials.

Explore Beef

http://explorebeef.org

This site offers information about the beef industry's compliance with environmental requirements, animal care, and safety. It also offers visitors an opportunity to read about beef farmers and ranchers in all fifty states and to learn about some of the latest innovations at farms and ranches in the United States.

Iowa State University Organic Agriculture

http://extension.agron.iastate.edu/organicag/

This website focuses on research and extension activities in organic agriculture, both on the farms and in universities. It includes news, frequently asked questions, and resources.

National FFA Organization (formerly Future Farmers of America)

https://www.ffa.org

For more than eighty years, the mission of this organization has been to help young people explore their interests in a broad range of agricultural careers. The organization focuses on the diversity of agriculture.

Organic.org

http://www.organic.org

The purpose of this website is to help educate people on the benefits of organic agriculture, food, and other products. A Product Review section and a Just for Kids section include organic games, kids' recipes, and a Just for Parents subsection.

WHITE PAPERS

Pew Commission on Industrial Farm Animal Production. *Putting Meat on the Table: Industrial Farm Animal Production in America.*" Washington, DC: Pew Charitable Trusts and Johns Hopkins Bloomberg School of Public Health, 2008.
The Pew Commission on Industrial Farm Animal Production conducts comprehensive, fact-based, and balanced examinations of key aspects of the farm animal industry.

INDEX

PHOTO ACKNOWLEDGMENTS

The images in this book are used with the permission of: AP Photo/Charles Dharapak, pp. 5-6; © Steven May/Alamy, p. 7; © fotog/Getty Images, p. 8; © Julia Schmalz/USA TODAY, pp. 12-13; © Imagno/Contributor/Hulton Archive/Getty Images, p. 14; Courtesy of The Soil Association, p. 17; © CORBIS, pp. 18, 52; © Co Rentmeester/Time Life Pictures/Getty Images, p. 19; © Wally McNamee/CORBIS, p. 23; © Matthew Staver/ The New York Times/Redux, pp. 26-27; © Janie McCarthy/2009 Getty Images, p. 30; © Brian Fitzgerald/Aurora Photos/CORBIS, p. 31; © Danny Gainer/USA TODAY, p. 33; © Jeff Greenberg/Alamy, p. 34; © Blend Images/SuperStock, pp. 38-39; © Eileen Blass/ USA TODAY, pp. 40, 95 (top); © H. Mark Weidman Photography/Alamy, p. 41; © Curt Maas/AGStock USA/Alamy, p. 46; © Sergej Razvodovskij/Shutterstock Images, p. 47; © Everett Collection/Alamy, pp. 50-51; © Maciej Dakowicz/Alamy, p. 54; Scott Bauer/ Agricultural Research Service, USDA, pp. 59, 61; © IndexStock/SuperStock, pp. 64-65; Photo courtesy Farm Sanctuary, p. 68; AP Photo/Goldman Environmental Foundation, Tom Dusenbery , p. 69; © Clive Streeter/Dorling Kindersley/Getty Images, p. 73; © Kathy Coatney/AGStock USA/Alamy, p. 74 (top); © Michael Chow/USA TODAY, p. 76 (bottom); © Wolfgang Flamisch/Corbis Cusp/Alamy, pp. 78-79; © George Steinmetz/ CORBIS, p. 81; © Patti McConville/Alamy, p. 85; © Julia Guest/David Hoffman Photo Library/Alamy, p. 86; © Jack Gruber/USA TODAY, pp. 90-91; © John Lee/Aurora Photos/Alamy, p. 93; © Todd Plih/USA TODAY, p. 100.

Front Cover: © Eileen Blass/USA TODAY.

Main body text set in USA TODAY Roman Regular 10.5/15.

ABOUT THE AUTHOR

Jack L. Roberts is a freelance author and editor who splits his time between Los Angeles, California, and Key West, Florida. He has written numerous nonfiction books for children and young adults.